Mike,

Do you believe in miracles?

I do! God is alive today and He has not changed. Miracles happen on a daily basis. The question you believe is, do loving in a rod?

THE HARD ROAD

WHAT IF ALMOST DYING WAS THE VERY THING THAT SAVED YOUR LIFE?

Michael S Pruett

MICHAEL S. PRUETT

WITH VANESSA J. CHANDLER

HEB 13:8

"I've known Michael Pruett for over three decades and can easily attest: he is the 'real deal!' Sometimes suffering brings new perspective to life, and Michael Pruett knows what it truly means to live! It was through his courageous fight for life that showed him the redemptive qualities of God and the miracles He is capable of. Michael's story is absolutely inspirational and begs the question: What are you living for?"

Dr. Joe White - *President, Kanakuk Ministries*

"The fact that Michael is here today to tell this story is proof that miracles still happen. You will be moved and blessed as you see the hand of God working to restore hope not only in Michael, but in the lives of those around him."

Chip Ingram - *Senior Pastor, Venture Christian Church*
Teaching Pastor, Living on the Edge

"In so many ways, Michael's story is the story of all of us. We need to learn how to be liberated from trusting in our own strength and ability so that we can learn to live a life of dependency on God.

Michael, a successful businessman, respected community leader, and avid sports enthusiast, learned this lesson through a serious accident that could have ended his life. Instead of a tragic tale, Michael's life has become an inspiring story of one man's journey to discover the limits of his own wisdom in order to more fully inherit the riches of God's grace. If pride was the root of man's fall, then humility is the pathway to redemption. Michael's journey to this discovery is a lesson to us all."

Mike Atkins - *Senior Pastor, River Crossing Church*

"Then Abraham lifted his eyes and looked, and there behind him was a ram caught in a thicket by its horns. So Abraham went and took the ram, and offered it up for a burnt offering instead of his son."

Genesis 22:13

Disclaimer: Although the events and facts included in this story are real, Red Arrow Media has taken creative license to dramatize some scenes, specifically those involving dreams and visions.

Paramedic Trent Jensen was hunched over a makeshift table in the radio room of one of Jackson Hole's six fire and emergency medical service stations, writing a report. He ran his fingers back-and-forth across his forehead in contemplation, his thumb pressed into his temple. Seated, his six-foot-four frame was still imposing, but off the job, his congenial demeanor and good-natured grin revealed a homegrown young man from the Midwest.

Thirteen hours of duty lay ahead of him and his team who relaxed on recliners around the room, resting from the day's events and already anticipating what the night might bring. Every twenty-four hour shift at the station followed the same routine: EMS and fire training at seven in the morning, physical exercise in the afternoon, then administrative duties and rest at night. Some days no calls came in, especially during the off-season, but of course it was impossible to anticipate. Their waiting game was endless. Adrenaline was always high. The knowledge that at any given time they'd have to make life-and-death decisions for someone was a weight that no one carried lightly.

Emergency calls could come in from four thousand square miles surrounding Jackson, and Trent was the designated leader of medical relief at the station. His team could be hiking in three feet of snow 10,000 feet up on the Grand Teton to rescue a waylaid tourist or rushing a few blocks away to administer help to someone suffering from a heart attack.

Tuning in for a moment to the conversation buzzing behind him, Trent looked up from his report and scanned the room, taking in the tired faces of his team and resting his gaze on Brian Carr. Brian was an honest, quick-witted friend and EMT that Trent could always count on to offer choice remarks.

"Well, that poor woman's cat will never get up on a roof again," Brian quipped. He was attempting to lighten the mood with a jovial comment about their last call.

Trent shook his head, relieving his heavy concentration. His colleagues often joked about what they called the "grandma calls." Those rescues were tediously uneventful, like saving stranded animals or scouring the basement due to a mysterious sound. These were unexpected calls, but sometimes they served as light-hearted breaks from more harrowing rescues. Before Trent could join in with a quip of his own, a burst of static noise erupted from the radio on his belt.

In an instant, the room fell silent as senses snapped into high alert, listening. The first thing Trent registered was the tone signaling the nature of the emergency. It was not a fire.

Then the voice came through. "Medic 10, this is Dispatch. Man on motorcycle collided with medium-sized truck on corner of 265 South Millward Street and West Hansen Avenue. First responders are recommending a CHARLIE response at this time. Repeat, CHARLIE response."

Trent felt as though the blood drained from his body—a familiar sensation. CHARLIE meant a potentially life-threatening scenario where time could affect the patient's wellbeing. "This is Medic 10. Roger that, Dispatch," Trent returned. "On our way."

Steadying his nerves, he signaled to his team with a glance and headed for the garage directly adjacent to the radio room, which housed two ambulances, a yellow wild land truck, and two fire trucks. The team had drilled procedures so many times that they didn't need to communicate. Amanda revved the engine of an ambulance while Trent and Brian cleared the steps to the right side door servicing the back of the rig. Five others jumped on one of the fire engines. Lights flashed above the oversized garage door of the station as it rose, releasing the team to their mission. They knew there was a man near death that they could possibly help, but there were no guarantees.

The multi-colored, beaming lights and screaming siren of Medic 10 blurred through the air as it sped to the accident just ten blocks from the station. Suddenly, another voice cut in on the dispatch line. "This is Medic 60. We were filling up nearby, so we are already en route. Repeat, we are already en route."

Recognizing Cori Neckels' voice, Trent exhaled in relief. Fifty-year-old Cori Neckels was an intermediate EMT with twenty years of experience. Often referred to as the station's "mom," her calm demeanor during an emergency gave the team confidence that things were being done correctly, and that everything would be okay.

As Amanda maneuvered the ambulance, Trent stared at the red and yellow lines running along the interior of the ambulance's double doors, grateful for an instant to steel his mind before entering the stress of another emergency. He had spent over two thousand hours training for moments like this. In fact, he lived for these moments. After nearly a decade of navigating through dangerous situations, he still looked forward to each day of work.

Trent prepared himself for the scene he knew he would soon be confronting and felt the familiar fear rise in his body. He unconsciously fingered the wooden cross that hung on a leather string beneath his uniform. A gift from his father, it helped steady his nerves when he faced how quickly and tragically life could end. Yet he also knew his training would kick in like a hallucinogenic drug, checking his emotions and channeling the adrenaline into tunnel vision that would help him make keen observations, identify problems, and administer solutions in a matter of seconds.

Camaraderie was essential to his team, and he implicitly trusted each member. They were not only trained to provide basic medical relief, but also to climb ladders to extract victims trapped in a fire, use an axe and a chainsaw, force entry into a burning and smoking building, break down a door or window, escape from entrapments, navigate in swift water in the wild, and enforce search-and-rescue tactics and hazard responses. They had seen and done it all, and most of them had witnessed death. Long after they had grieved these tragedies, the memories lived on, even in their dreams, fueling their vigilance and determination to be ready for the next emergency. They all knew it wasn't just a job—it was a lifestyle.

The ambulance slowed suddenly, coming to a halt in front of Snake River Brewing Company, a pub on the corner of Millward and Hansen.

Trent swung open the side door of the ambulance while Amanda hustled for the gurney, and Brian for the rig's exterior compartment. An audience had formed in the pub's parking lot. Trained to analyze the details of every scene, Trent immediately noticed the presence of one of his station's captains. The captain was off duty and dressed down, and Trent made the split-second assumption he had been eating at the pub.

Trent acknowledged the captain as he jumped down from the rig. The fire engine following behind them blocked the road. The rest of the station's EMTs sprang out and headed toward the crowd of people.

As the lead paramedic, a job that required a high level of intense training beyond EMT status, Trent would assess what the first responders were already doing, and in about ten seconds, decipher how best to manage the scene. The wellbeing of a patient was on his watch. If he failed, the patient's life could end.

Trent's eyes met a gruesome sight. A man's battered body lay on the pavement. A thick circle of blood surrounded a gaping wound in his head, a mess of skin and sinew. The right half of his scalp had peeled off from his skull and lay beside him. The patient was already combative. His writhing arms scraped the asphalt as he reached out in front of him. He mumbled an incomprehensible name. His legs jolted as if coursing with electricity.

John Doe. Trent noticed that the man, despite being mangled within a horrific scene, looked vaguely familiar.

The woman stationed at John Doe's head was the wife of the captain he had noted seconds before; she was a battalion chief. Trent determined that she had most likely been having dinner with her husband at the pub across the street, heard the frightening cacophony from the accident, and rushed to become one of the first responders at the site. She was already administering a manual C-spine immobilization to keep the patient's head still and neck straight.

Behind him, Trent heard the outside compartment of the ambulance slam shut. Brian was towing the yellow plastic backboard that would hold the patient's body. Trent's mental timer began. He had been at the scene only three seconds.

The petite frame of Cori Neckels from Medic 60, who had radioed Trent's team while in route, was crouched and leaning over the patient's right side, assessing his back. She cut the man's shirt to expose probable wounds and gently dug a hand beneath him over the line of his spine. She bit down hard on her lower lip, a nervous habit.

"He's not responding to anyone yet. He could be seizing," Trent shouted as he ran toward the scene.

Five seconds.

He scanned the area to see if the team had missed any other patients. A man sat in the bed of an older truck, shaking his head, as if in shock. Trent knew without asking that this man was responsible for hitting the patient. His wounds, which appeared to be minor, were being treated.

Trent arrived at John Doe's body in seven seconds.

JULY 15, 2012
HIGHWAY 191
13:35 MT

Michael Pruett gunned his black and chrome Bonneville T100 into gear and maneuvered onto the highway. Before gaining speed, he glanced over his shoulder at Dawn, his wife of two years. Her deep aqua-green eyes met his gaze as she cozied her petite figure up behind his solid six-foot-four frame.

The ride to the park from the church was a short distance, and Michael barely had enough time to enjoy the wind against his face before slowing down his James Dean replica. Dawn jumped down from the bike and attempted to straighten and reshape her honey-colored hair without a mirror. Then she smoothed out her dark blue jeans that tucked into tall brown boots.

Noting Dawn's effort, Michael commented, "You look fine." Head and shoulders above his wife, he was proud to walk arm-in-arm with her, a classic American beauty who still caught the attention of a passerby.

Her cheeks were flushed from the summer sun and still full enough to give her the appearance of a much younger woman. Not only that, she was confident and professional. Combined with her beauty, those traits continually captivated him.

"You look great, actually," Michael corrected himself.

"Too late," she said, giving him a coveted, pretty smile. She quickly turned her attention to the people they were approaching.

"There you are!" came a recognizable voice behind them. Matt Deehan's Boston Irish accent was easy to place in Wyoming. His rugged figure towered over Dawn, much like Michael's. As usual, his salt and pepper curls lay unkempt, and he wore a wry smile. "I thought you guys either got lost or decided to head on home."

"We might have gotten turned around once," Dawn jested.

"No, no," Michael answered in mock defensiveness, "I just like to take the long route."

"Oh, is that what it is," Deehan stated in obvious amusement. "And sometimes you like to take the very, *very* long route." He rolled his eyes exclusively for Dawn before giving her a wink. It was a boyish gesture, but it had its intended effect.

Dawn laughed in spite of herself, and Michael shook his head as she let go of his arm, releasing him to make his way around the entire crowd. During their three-year relationship, Dawn had learned that meeting new people, having great conversations, and catching up with friends enabled her husband to come alive. At times others saw Michael's outgoing, sociable nature as a form of social climbing, or—as his stepdaughters considered it—annoying. Michael didn't mind and he certainly didn't change. He simply enjoyed people. In the same way Dawn encouraged his social freedom,

Michael understood that although she could appear as an energetic people-person, she was a textbook introvert. She appreciated listening more than speaking and the personal over the public in almost every case.

"Hey there," Matt Somers, one of Michael's close friends, said as the couple approached his picnic table. "Take a seat." Somers' wife, Heidi, sat beside him, and one of his children was enthusiastically clamoring on his back. Like most of Michael's friends, Somers was noticeably athletic and donned his usual red baseball cap. The three friends known collectively by their last names, Pruett, Deehan, and Somers, had traveled to many sports games in celebration of their fanaticism.

Dawn made herself comfortable. "There are so many people here! I'm surprised you haven't taken off on a visiting mission, Michael."

"Don't worry," Deehan whispered to Dawn loudly enough for everyone to hear. "He's already mentally orbiting the planet!"

Dawn glared blithely at Deehan and Somers laughed.

"Oh come on, you guys," Christina Feuz cut in as she stood up. Christina was Dawn's ever-smiling small group leader from church. She and her husband, Dan, sat next to the Somers clan. "Give Michael a break!" she declared, clutching her newborn with one arm while reaching over to playfully pat Michael's back with the other. "Poor Michael." She motioned for Dawn to go with her to get a plate of food. "This little one's finally ready for me to eat."

Michael shook his head and laughed as the two women rose from the table. He was used to the incessant teasing.

As Dawn passed him, she gave her husband a quick, nearly imperceptible, coy look.

Deehan joined in. "Yeah, yeah. Poor Michael. Cruising in on his motorcycle with his trophy wife. God knows I'm still looking for mine."

"I married for love, not looks," Michael quipped in return.

"No, that's what Dawn did," Deehan jeered.

Somers chuckled, and Michael grabbed Deehan's shoulder as if to pick a fight.

"That was my plan too…" Deehan added quietly with derision.

All present unintentionally heard Deehan's comment and the table became unexpectedly quiet.

Michael added awkwardly, "I should at least get something to eat before I sit down." Spying the location of food, his eyes strayed to Richard Lewis, a new colleague at his firm, Jackson Hole Real Estate Associates. Richard looked casual yet somehow debonair in his fresh jeans and crisp white shirt. His white hair and gray, neatly trimmed beard stood out in the crowd. Michael's stomach tensed. Maybe he wasn't that hungry after all.

Richard caught Michael's look and lifted up his cup of iced tea to greet him from across the lawn.

Michael acknowledged him with a single nod. Before Richard joined the company, he and Michael had been rivals in the real estate game. At one point, when both men went after the same sale, things got heated. Richard had lifted his hand to him on that day as well…only to defend himself against the threat of Michael's swinging fist.

Decades had passed since Michael was in an actual, old-fashioned fight, and his reaction caught everyone off guard, including himself. He had accused Richard of trying to steal one of his potentially lucrative deals, and since Richard had already landed a number of important clients that year, Michael wasn't about to lose a sizeable and much-needed commission without a fight. Thankfully, someone—Michael could never remember who—restrained him. In his mind, Michael could still see the look on Richard's face, his bewildered and slightly amused expression. It still shamed and infuriated him. If Richard had gotten physical in return, who would have come out on top? Richard could have, at the very least, let him win that one.

Their relationship now, though a little distant, was at least cordial. It had to be. They were in too many of the same circles. Michael knew how to be friendly with anyone, even a competitor, despite the undertone of resentment he still felt when he noted Richard's professional success. Although he hated to admit it, Richard was a great agent and a convincing seller—especially for ranches and resorts. Michael had tried to analyze Richard's success on numerous occasions. Perhaps it was because he gave off the essence of a real cowboy, a man that looked more like a character out of a classic western novel rather than the typical stuffed suit selling real estate. Whatever it was, Richard came across as strong and reliable, and buyers sensed it.

"Why the sour look, man?" Somers nudged, noting the change in Michael's face.

"You're coming over to watch the Cardinals on Wednesday, right?" Michael inquired, ignoring the question.

"Yeah, of course," he answered.

Michael flashed him a friendly, if somewhat forced, smile. He suddenly felt exhausted. He had the urge to get out of there, to hop back on his motorcycle and drive the familiar route to Yellowstone National Park. He and Dawn had planned on leaving the picnic early anyway and a ride through the landscape might be just enough to keep his mind at rest. If they left now, they could be back in time to meet their friends for dinner as planned.

"Sounds good," Michael said, turning his attention back to the table. "I'm gonna go get Dawn, maybe head out a little early." He spotted her in a conversation with Nathan Ver Burg, a new board member at River Crossing Church.

Setting down his drink, Deehan raised his hands in the air. "You haven't even eaten yet!"

"I'll grab something on the way out," he called back over his shoulder to a confused Deehan.

Michael's lengthy form and determined gait was hard to miss as he approached his wife from across the lawn.

Dawn looked up from her conversation, and he could tell that she interpreted his intent immediately.

"I think we are heading out," she explained to Nathan.

She would be as relieved as her husband to spend time away from the crowd.

B ased on the team's efforts and John Doe's reactions, Trent knew the man had been severely traumatized, which meant his spine had been affected. The chances of a successful rescue with patient recovery were dwindling rapidly.

Cori was talking to the victim, attempting to gauge his consciousness. "Wake up! Wake up, Sir!"

John Doe's words were becoming clearer, "Wi...wife...."

The plea resonated within Trent. Was the family close by? He had seen too many of those moments. Past accident scenes soared through his internal lens, almost all with the same harrowing effect—a father arriving at the accident in time to see his son take a final breath; a mother screaming as her child's body hung halfway out the windshield. Those were the images that stuck with him even years later, that came back to him in moments like these and had to be forced away.

"All right," Trent belted out. "What do you guys have?"

Cori's raw green eyes bore up at him. She seemed just as relieved to see him as he was to see her. "Single patient. Unconscious at first. Consciousness level is now a six, maybe seven. Primary wounds in the head only. Response to pain. Back is clear."

"Okay. His skin is pink, warm, dry. Good signs."

Brian reached the battalion chief's position and took over. Now at the head of the body, he became the designated leader reporting to Trent. He felt the skull for fractures. Cori knelt on the stranger's left side and handed Brian saline to clean the head laceration. Scarlet blood spilled over Brian's hands as he rinsed the wound and placed a large white 4x4 inch gauze inside it to stop the bleeding. For now, they'd have to leave the gash open as they found it. Only a nurse or doctor was authorized to staple the skin back together over his skull.

Before the off-duty battalion chief walked back to the lingering crowd, Trent overheard her say, "He was just lying here when we arrived. There was so much blood that no one wanted to touch him."

Trent prodded his team further, "Rapid trauma assessment?"

Cori refocused on the patient and pulled up his eyelids, then measured his pulse. "Breathing and pulse are good."

Brian piped in, "Broken ankle. Minor abrasions on left arm, right arm, and legs. Nueros intact all around."

John Doe's arms shot out again. "Wife...my wife!" He was reacting to head trauma. EMTs would often compare the human brain to a computer's hard drive. When the computer crashed, it had to reboot. This man's brain was restarting.

As Cori tried to pin him down to put an oxygen line into his nose, he gripped her arms. He appeared to be about six-foot-four with a sturdy build. She and Brian wrestled with him to keep him subdued. If he moved too much, the abrasion on his head would no doubt worsen.

Possible subluxation, Trent realized. The victim's vertebrae were probably misaligned, and the chance of recovery minimal.

"We need to get ready to lift the patient onto the backboard," Brian interjected, breathing heavily.

"Roger that," Cori replied, gasping as the stranger swung his fist toward her face. "Some hindrance here!" After managing to somewhat contain the patient, Cori announced, "On your count, Brian, we're going to move him as a unit."

Brian nodded. "One, two, three." Together, they carefully lifted the patient onto the plastic backboard. Brian held his neck while he velcroed the blue and yellow c-collar to keep him from further damage.

Trent noted the man's closed eyes and verbal incoherence, estimating that his level of consciousness was rising, but still not much above the lowest level of three.

"We're going to run Code 3. I'll give a report to Saint John's Hospital. Rapid transport," Trent decided.

"Copy that," Brian answered.

"Saint John's. Medic 10." Trent waited for a response.

"Go ahead, Medic 10," a voice rang out from the walkie-talkie in Trent's hand.

"Saint John's, be advised we have a Trauma Red patient. Approximately forty-five year-old male. Patient was on a motorcycle. Hit by a truck. No helmet. Scalp avulsion, right side. About half of his scalp. Possible open skull fracture. Subluxation of spine. There is profuse bleeding at this time.

We're controlling it. ETA five minutes."

"Roger that, Medic 10. Room One is being prepped."

As Brian and Cori strapped down the unrelenting man, Trent tried to gauge his awareness. "Sir, can you tell me your name?"

Conscious enough to understand what was being asked of him, the man began mouthing a word, only managing to make an unintelligible sound.

Trent repeated his question twice before he got a clear answer.

"Pru...Pru...Pruett." The name sounded familiar, but Trent couldn't place it.

"Pruett, tell us what happened."

No response.

Brian, who was gripping the man's hand, commanded, "Pruett, pull on my hand."

The patient managed a small tug.

Cori was finally able to place the oxygen line in Pruett's nose.

"Okay, Pruett," Brian coached him. "Take big, deep breaths for me."

The man's eyes fluttered open momentarily.

"Excellent. Lungs sound clear, both sides."

Cori cut in, "Hey, Buddy. We're taking you to the hospital. You got hurt."

Trent started toward the back of the rig. "I'll get things set up."

Brian, Cori, and Amanda gripped the sides of the backboard through the handholds, lifted the patient smoothly onto the gurney, and wheeled him toward the ambulance doors. From inside, Trent gestured that he was ready for them to load the gurney. Brian gave a thumb's up, and the gurney jolted up and inward. Cori climbed in after it and settled on Pruett's right side. Brian jumped in next to Cori, and Amanda clambered into the driver's seat.

Brian caught Trent's eye. "He kept saying 'Pruett.' He doesn't know what happened. I don't know what his first name is, but I think it's Michael. I've seen him advertise property a few times. He does real estate in town."

Trent looked down at his patient. First names are better, but personal. *John Doe* is just a body; *Michael* is a life.

"Michael, you're still with me, right? Squeeze my hand."

"Still has a good grip," Trent reported. His focus now was to keep Michael breathing well. He reached out for Michael's left hand and clamped on a finger monitor to measure his heart rate and oxygen saturation. Bright lines on the monitor's screen came to life, rising and falling with his bodily rhythms. Trent wrapped the inflatable upper bicep cuff over Michael's right arm to read his blood pressure. Iridescent lines jolted upward above the other lines on the screen.

The time read 5:35—only seven minutes since the call.

The ride to the park and back took several hours, yet the familiar route never got old, and Michael and Dawn enjoyed it whenever they could. A perfect tapestry of nature, Teton County and its surroundings covered ninety square miles, ninety-seven percent of which had been set aside as National Park and wildlife reserves. Often called "God's country," this stretch of land was too beautiful not to experience every day as if for the first time. Before them on the left, the Teton mountain range rose above the basin in haunting majesty. Its peaks—like razor-sharp teeth— still bore white masses of snow in the warm weather.

As Michael accelerated down the highway, Dawn wrapped her arms more tightly around his waist, and his mouth curved upward in a smile. He attempted to give himself to the ride—just the two of them in the warmth, floating past white-capped mountains and grassy plains where elk and bison idly grazed. No dramatic teenage stepdaughters, no demands from work. It was a bluebird day, not a cloud in the sky, which was typical for short summer months in Jackson. The rest of the year the city was entrenched in some form of winter.

The couple stopped for a moment to enjoy the view of the Snake River from an overlook. At Moran Junction, Michael turned left onto the John D. Rockefeller Jr. Parkway and passed through Colter Bay Village, where the river spilled into the looming waters of Jackson Lake. They could see visitors and locals filling the marina, eager to sail in the fair weather.

As they rode on, the mountains and lake subsided into drier, open plains. Michael's mind drifted back to his current conundrum. Not one to believe in luck, he couldn't help but consider that he needed some kind of break. He gritted his teeth in frustration. When he had jumped into real estate five years earlier—after conquering several start-ups, flipping houses, and just about everything else a successful entrepreneur might do—real estate seemed to be another venture guaranteed to thrive. Property in Jackson had jumped an astronomical 513% between 1992 and 2007. Baby boomers were arriving, looking for recreational paradise or a second home. But like the rest of the economy, the market crashed and by 2008, sales slowed to the lowest in twenty-five years. The excitement and creativity involved in matching property with buyer kept him in the game, yet the lack of financial return cost him everything. He had arrived at the lowest, most humbling season of his life.

His ego had tanked along with the real estate market. Everything he had worked for since starting over after moving to Jackson nearly seventeen years before was eroding in front of him like an ebbing tide. There was nothing he could do to stop it. For the first time in his life, he had been questioning his ability to do *anything* well. It seemed like he had the opposite effect of King Midas—instead of turning the things he touched to gold, his touch caused things to disintegrate. At times, he wanted to tell his clients they would have more success with someone else. He had risen high…and then fallen hard. As things in real estate had spiraled downward, he knew it was bigger than just a market crash. He needed to end this—whatever "this" was—once and for all.

The truth was that he was nearly broke, and he felt like he was back to the beginning of his career again. Dawn's salary supported their expenses, but with Dawn on a recent sabbatical, would he be able to support the whole family? It was a bothersome question to which he had not found the answer. Somewhere he had gone wrong. Somewhere money had become more than a means to an end; money *was* the end. Perhaps he hadn't started out that way, but who knew? All Michael remembered was a fleeting feeling of confidence when he first began his career. His star was rising and he had nowhere to go but up. How long ago was that? He couldn't place it. Twenty-one-year old Michael flashed in his mind, shaming him.

Then there was college Michael. *Yeah,* he thought sarcastically. *Follow your dreams. You're heading places.* Suddenly—and uninvited— Rachel came to mind. He witnessed a brief scene of happiness…a blanket on the grass at a movie in the park. Younger Michael had somehow chased her away, and he still hadn't figured out how he had done it.

He felt Dawn grip more tightly and looked down to check his speed. He cleared his throat and shifted gears to slow down.

He had always considered himself a good, Christian, all-American man. When he was younger, he kept a tattered scrap of paper that his father gave him that read, "God Never Changes." After his first few setbacks and disappointments in early adulthood, Michael placed that paper in his wallet, choosing not to look at it for many years. *God may not change, but life does constantly.* Michael leaned into God in a traditional sense, but he also believed that man must take independent action to secure his future. Being able to claim his success and be responsible for his faults was something that lent him confidence. But lately in quiet moments when Michael's mind was still and his thoughts turned against him, he wondered if God was actually the problem. Was God teaching him a lesson? If so, what?

Michael would work on it. He'd fix it. He knew he had to. His parents had brought him up in faith and also championed the spirit of self-reliance, and he was well versed in how to pick himself up by his bootstraps. It was a legacy he embraced, but the thought of having to fix some unseen, unknown problem exhausted him. If God were against him, what would be the point? Couldn't God let him win just once? He exhaled and unknowingly gained speed, keeping his eyes focused on the yellow lines on the road before him.

The couple reached their turnaround point, the south entrance of Yellowstone National Park. Michael slowed the motorcycle and killed the engine. They stepped off the bike and stretched their legs, looking out over grassy knolls on their left and the blue expanse of Yellowstone Lake to their right.

Dawn could sense that he had unwittingly become tense and looked up at him in question.

"Just thinking about work, but I'm stopping now," Michael responded, reaching out to grab her and hold her close.

"Love," Dawn began, smoothing her windblown hair and attempting to change the subject so as to distract him. "I'm not up for doing anything else tonight. I've been feeling guilty about it, but I'm hoping something else comes up so we don't have to go out."

He shook his head in jest. Michael didn't believe in canceling anything, particularly dinner plans.

She simply grinned cajolingly back at him, and, of course, it worked.

He laughed at how easily she could sway him. "Maybe they canceled." He reached down, grabbed his phone, and checked his email. A new message from a local realtor appeared in his inbox.

Michael,

I have someone who'd like to see one of the properties you've listed, The Lofts. Are you available this afternoon?

Situated just three blocks from the town square in arguably the best location in Jackson, the property boasted high-end residential condominiums. Small in square footage, they offered affordable options for the average buyer. Red brick exteriors furnished a different feel than most of the town's cowboy-style log cabins. Several of the condominiums had already sold and were still showing well.

Michael internalized the possibility in anticipation. The property had potential for great revenue. "Looks like I've got a showing. We should probably head back."

Dawn frowned and then punched him playfully in mild annoyance. Their lovely afternoon was being cut short, and they'd probably go to dinner with their friends after all. "Well, at least let me change shoes!"

she teased.

"All right, I'll drop you at home, show the property, and then pick you up."

She climbed on behind him, and he revved the engine.

JULY 15, 2012

AMBULANCE EN ROUTE

17:37 MT

"Can you blink your eyes three times for me?" Trent asked. "You were in a motorcycle accident, and we're taking you to the hospital."

"There's significant bleeding here!" Brian exclaimed as he swathed Michael's head again with new gauze.

Trent lost count of the number of bandages Michael had bled through. Each gauze lasted only a few seconds.

The beeping from the medical equipment, the individual voices barking out the patient status, and the immediacy of the responding movements filled the small interior of the ambulance with a sharp sense of anxiety. Checking to see if Michael's consciousness level was rising, Trent shifted his gaze to the patient's face. "Michael. Tell me what hurts right now."

"My...head...hurts," Michael stuttered. He struggled against the straps that held him down, but his entire body was immobilized.

"Cori, go ahead and get an IV on that side to keep his organs perfused. I'll monitor fluids to keep head pressure in check." Trent called to Amanda, "Run Code 3."

Brian cut in, "I've got a second set of lung sounds. Still strong on both sides."

"Okay," Trent confirmed. "I'm going to get blood pressure on this side and then start an IV on the other."

The machine analyzed Pruett's body, the lines racing and weaving up and down.

"Oxygen at 98%. Pulse is about 110. Getting blood pressure," Trent continued.

"Bleeding is starting to slow down," Brian interjected while still applying pressure.

The machine beeped three times. "BP is 120/70. Not too high. That's good." Trent exhaled.

Cori announced, "Line's going good on this side. I'm running wide open."

Trent scanned the surroundings. "Almost to Saint John's. Pruett, squeeze my hand for me. Okay, tell me what finger I'm pinching...good."

The ambulance skidded to halt at Saint John's emergency entrance at 5:38.

Michael loved Dawn for many reasons, but he appreciated her supportive attitude most of all. By the time they met, he was forty-one, and his financial situation had already become difficult. Michael had asked her to marry him in spite of his insecurity. After she replied with an exuberant, "Yes," declaring that he was the perfect man for her, he met her gaze and joked, "I know you're not marrying me for money, because my tax return shows that I'm at poverty level."

Michael and Dawn reached their house on Pine Drive overlooking downtown Jackson at half past four. Michael slowed and circled around the cul-de-sac at the end of the street and gunned the motorcycle up their steep driveway.

Willie, Michael's longhaired golden retriever—loyally awaiting their return—bounded up to greet them.

As he idled the engine, Dawn stepped off the bike and leaned over to kiss him. "Good luck!"

Michael reached down to ruffle Willie's fur and then said, "Be back in a bit."

Dawn hesitated. Her gaze strayed back to him again, uncertain.

"Something wrong, Love?"

"You don't want to take your helmet?"

"Nah!" Michael chortled. "I never do in town."

Dawn stared at him a moment longer and shook her head before she turned and stepped up the pathway to their front door.

Michael knew Dawn sensed things—things no one else would know—about people or situations that weren't quite right. Her intuition was rarely wrong. He didn't understand her all the time, but he had learned to listen. Seeing as she hadn't made too much of it this time, however, he put it aside.

He shifted gears and glided down their driveway, curving around the hills of Pine Drive and turning onto South Millward Street. The drive to the condos was an easy one-mile ride. Five minutes later, he was there. The showing went by quickly as well, and the realtor and client were cordial and interested. He knew there were no promises, but at least it was something.

He checked his watch to make sure he was still on time to get Dawn for dinner. It was almost 5:30. They would be a little late. He climbed back on his bike, started the engine, and took off toward West Broadway, slowing as he neared the evening rush of downtown. Once on the home stretch, he accelerated to twenty-five miles per hour.

As he cruised down South Millward toward the upcoming intersection at West Hansen, he barely noticed the older, full-sized truck speeding toward him in the opposite lane. Normally he was more alert to large vehicles, but his mind was full, and he had the right of way. Snake River Brewery loomed ahead on the corner. No doubt it would be filled with off duty cops and other personnel who were either gearing up or winding down for another Monday.

His thoughts briefly flickered back on Dawn's precautionary moment, and he had only a second to register that the truck was not slowing as it neared the intersection. Before he could react, it was swerving into a wide left turn—directly in front of him. Michael yelled out, but there was no time to stop. They were going to crash head on. He instinctively laid down his bike. The side of his body and limbs dragged along the pavement, forming deep gashes that instantly spurted vibrant red blood. The rusted paint of the old F-150 flashed in front of his eyes as he hit the truck's fender headfirst.

As his mind began to darken, his limp body slithered underneath the truck. A long screech of grating metal filled the air as the truck crushed everything beneath it. The truck spun out of control, dragging him with it, and finally grated to a stop in front of the brewery, its front end ground into the concrete.

Michael knew that he was about to die, but that did not concern him in comparison to his final question. Where was Dawn? He could hear his own voice calling out for her and tried to lift his head to find her, but couldn't.

Then there was only silence.

D awn couldn't shake it, the feeling that was both familiar and unnerving. She could tell herself that nothing was wrong, but she knew something wasn't quite right either.

Michael hadn't answered her calls or texts.

She unconsciously bit her lower lip and furiously typed another text on her phone, not able to dislodge the image of Michael on his bike or the uneasy sensation that accompanied it. As if to confirm the feeling, the sound of an ambulance siren spiraled upward through the air, reaching their cabin on the mountainside. She felt her stomach lurch in response.

It can't be him. It simply can't be him, she reasoned, yet she found herself running to the bathroom, sick from nerves. From somewhere in Dawn's psyche came the memory of a recent nightmare. Someone—or *something*—had seized her neck with spindly, grotesque hands, choking her, threatening to hurt her three daughters. She couldn't move or scream and woke up shivering, a thin layer of sweat covering her face and tears tracking down her flushed cheeks. Her neck was sore to the touch as though she had bruised it. Michael woke to an empty bed and followed the sound of Dawn crying into the bathroom.

"Dawn?" he mumbled, his eyes trying to find her in the darkness.

"My girls," she started, and then erupted into gasping sobs. "He said he's going to come after my girls!"

"Who?" Michael asked, wrapping his arms around her and drawing her back to lean against him.

Dawn just kept sobbing, unable to answer.

Now she found herself rummaging through her makeup bag with shaking hands, nervously praying and desperately trying to push the memory away from her mind. "Can this really be happening after all we've come through together? I *can't* lose him!"

Dawn had always known that something wholly outside of herself, forces of evil and good, were constantly at work. She often heard of it referred to as Karma, but that was too passive, too reliant on her actions. When she married Michael just two years before, she had someone to talk with about her spiritual insight for the first time in her life. She had been uncharacteristically vulnerable with him. Even if Michael didn't have similar premonitions, he knew how to protect and comfort her when she needed it. Prior to Michael, these mystical and strange experiences would have turned other people in her circle away. She could feel the pull of that spiritual tension within her at this moment.

Raised a Mormon, Dawn adopted Michael's Christian beliefs on their first camping trip together. That night, wrapped tightly in their sleeping bags, they had lain on their backs and gazed at the stars. Michael asked her a simple question, one she had heard several times before without much consideration.

"What will happen when you die?"

Dawn didn't hesitate. "I will go to Heaven."

"How do you know?" He persisted.

"I believe in God."

"Well, Dawn, even the devil believes in God."

The memory caused her body to tremble. Each time she had retold the story, the emphasis had always been on her change of mind, her conversion. Now, the only part she could recall was that one, fated question.

She shook her head and, surprised by the tears that were falling onto her chest, dabbed her runny mascara with a tissue. She was unused to this side of herself. Life had forced her to become strong. Her daughters called her a rock for good reason.

What will happen if he dies? She wondered, the words feeling like lead in her stomach. Attempting to wash away her anxiety, Dawn splashed her face with water and brushed her teeth.

"Keep getting ready," she told herself. She slid on the outfit and shoes she had picked for the night out. Combing through her shoulder-length hair, her large eyes stared back at her in the mirror. They looked lost and worried.

"Good grief, Dawn. Get it together," she coaxed herself. Just an hour before she had felt carefree. She methodically moved the lipstick along the shape of her lips. Finishing, she found herself hurriedly dialing her middle child's number on the landline. Her three daughters were with their father in Green River, Wyoming, for the summer.

Paige answered on the second ring. They had already spoken earlier that afternoon, and after a few moments of silence, Paige asked why she was calling back.

"I think Michael…I think something might have happened to him."

"What do you mean?" Paige was used to her mother's intuition though she never understood it.

"It's just that I heard sirens. He's late. He won't answer his phone. I think he got in an accident."

"Okay, well…you don't *know* that."

In her mind, Dawn could see her daughter's face. Her forehead would be creased, her lips puckered due to biting her cheek in contemplation.

"I don't know for sure," she responded, "but I have this awful feeling."

"Calm down. I'm sure it's fine. He probably just left his phone somewhere. Or his bike."

Dawn sensed the humor in her middle daughter's words but was not amused. "Not this time," she said. Michael's relationship with his stepdaughters—namely Paige—was tenuous. Despite—or perhaps because of—his deep desire to be the perfect new stepdad and help instill good moral practices in their home, Michael hadn't been able to secure solid, carefree relationships with the girls.

"This time?" Paige answered. "He forgot the freaking tent on our camping trip. He could forget a phone."

Memories played through her mind. They were nebulous, a two-year-old blended family still struggling to reach a happy equilibrium. The situation with Paige and Michael had become a strange family joke, an event that seemed distant and barely recognizable, yet it was recent and real. What if something had happened to Michael? What would happen to her girls?

A normal sophomore in high school has bad days, but that first year living with Michael, Paige had bad months. Michael wanted her to join them at church each Sunday, and she could not bear another minute of forced morality with her stepfather. In a rebellious outburst, she snapped and went on a mini-stealing spree. After being caught, she was held in a back office at a local store, and forced to wait until Dawn and the last person Paige wanted to see—Michael—came to claim her. The security guard stood by while the newly established parental pair lectured her about her unethical values and poor decision-making.

Paige twisted in her chair as if being physically tortured, then stared at the floor in deaf defiance.

When Dawn finally finished the public scolding, she firmly stated, "Paige, go get in the car."

With this, Paige hopped from her seat and took off in a surprising sprint through the store and into the street.

Grabbing Dawn's arm, Michael shouted, "I'm getting the car!" He drove wildly to catch her, bumping over curbs and crushing green lawns. By the time they skidded into their garage, Paige had already sped into the house and locked herself in the bathroom. A fitting conclusion to her dramatic rage, she swallowed a bottle of pain medication and screamed through the door, "I would rather *die* than live another day with Michael!"

Dawn was appalled, but Michael was undaunted and burst through the door to stop her. Paige's hair was already mangled and wet from her emotional tirade. Michael was stunned by her condition, and in a frenzy, forced her to throw up. Somewhere in the blur of events, Paige bit him.

Later at the hospital when she came to, she saw the cuts and strange marks on Michael's hand. "What'd you do?" she remarked while pointing toward his wounds.

"Oh, that? A sixteen-year-old girl tried to bite my hand off."

Paige moved in with her father shortly after that incident, and hadn't come home since. Her anger toward Michael was still unresolved.

Dawn sighed and breathed in deeply. The siren outside was growing louder, but she chose to ignore it. Her middle child was strongly opinionated in most things, and in that moment, she adopted Paige's perspective to help her think straight. She broke into a half-hearted laugh, hoping to distract herself.

"I'm sure if he had been in an accident, the hospital would have called you," Paige continued.

As though in an answer to her daughter's words, the *call-waiting* feature beeped on Dawn's landline. Dawn lowered the phone and glanced at the identification. Blinking twice, she made sure she was reading it correctly.

Saint John's Hospital.

Her body suddenly felt cold, lifeless.

"Paige, I have to go!" She heard herself scream into the phone. "It's Saint John's." She managed to answer the other line, her fingers clumsy and unsteady. "Hello?" she asked, fearing the response.

"Mrs. Michael Pruett?" A voice asked.

"Yes."

"This is Saint John's. We need to inform you that your husband, Michael, has been in an accident."

Her throat was dry. She couldn't formulate words.

"We need you to come here immediately."

She remained silent.

"Mrs. Pruett? Hello?"

The woman addressed someone else in the background, her hand covering the earpiece to muffle it. Dawn could still hear her. "I think she might be in shock," the woman said. Then she spoke again. "Mrs. Pruett, is there someone else who can drive you?"

"Is he okay?" She finally whispered, breathless.

"He is alive, but we are not at liberty to disclose any more information at this time. We need you or another family member to come here immediately to release him for proper medical care."

"There's no one else," she stated flatly. The voice carried on, but Dawn couldn't comprehend her words. The phone clattered to the floor. Her body sunk downward and suddenly her hand was covering her mouth, trying to muffle the scream that was escaping from her carefully painted lips.

```
┌─────────────────────────────┐
│   SOUTH MiLLWARD AND         │
│   HANSEN AVENUE              │
│                             │
│   SCENE OF THE ACCIDENT     │
│        17:26 MT             │
└─────────────────────────────┘
```

How long had everything been black? Michael didn't know. The darkness slowly dissipated, and a pure, undiluted light began to surround him. He tried to open his eyes, but couldn't. Instead, he was suspended in white, a quiet balance of space and time. The nothingness was calm. He felt safe from the darkness there. Perhaps he would stay.

Unfamiliar voices came suddenly to him, disturbing the air. They spoke his name from under water, or perhaps from far away. Yet their reverberations felt near. Who were they, and why couldn't he see them? This time his eyes opened, and the brightness remained, shocking him. He squinted as if acid had penetrated his eyelids and scalded his pupils, and he winced away from the sharpness.

The brilliant white reminded him of something. Another place, another time. *My father saw that light. There—in his car.*

He heard a voice call to him again. Was that deep, muffled tone from his father?

"I have something to tell you," he heard his father say.

Michael whipped his head to the side, attempting to catch a glimpse of the fleeting ghost of a voice. Then he saw his father clearly—a respectable man with a bald spot, a set jaw, refined cheekbones, and a rigid nose. He sat there beside him in his old forest-green station wagon. Somehow, instinctively, Michael knew they were driving home from one of his many baseball games.

"Son, I don't know how to explain it, but I think I experienced a vision from God. Everything you were talking about earlier...I believe you."

Michael didn't understand, but he felt relieved anyway, like waking from a nightmare after unintentionally falling asleep. Everything was calm again. Outside of his passenger window, the rolling, forested hills on the back roads of Missouri maintained their lush green and muted yellow beauty. Beyond each small hill rose a branching tree or a bend in the river that cascaded over rocks and dense undergrowth. All appeared new, vibrant, and evergreen as though he had never seen it before.

"Okay, Dad," he heard himself say. His voice sounded young. How old was he? Michael could barely remember what his father was talking about.

"Something happened to me," he heard his father continue. "I was close to home on Clayton Road, just passing the fire station when my vision suddenly blurred. A yellow, greenish light filled the space all around me...almost like an aura. Then everything became black, and I saw a window. Someone drew the blinds apart, and a blinding light flooded everything around me, like it was a part of me. I know I sound crazy, but..."

His father hesitated. "I heard the word *Believe* with my own ears, clear as day, and then suddenly I was just sitting there in my car again like normal."

Michael saw his father's eyes then. His look was firm, yet compassionate. "Everything you learned this summer, Michael, it's true!"

Michael couldn't place the context. What had he learned? He opened his mouth to ask, but no words came out. What was he going to say? He couldn't recall.

"Dad, I believe you," he whispered over and over again. "I believe you." But his father's face dimmed, becoming hazy, and then disappeared.

No, please, come back! Michael heard himself call inside. Why couldn't he speak it out loud? His memory was jammed up with a mixture of sound and blurred images. A different vehicle came into view. The lights blared toward him again. Squirming in the luminescence, he tried to tell his father that he wasn't crazy.

He heard a voice ask for his name. Was it his father again? No, the voice was loud and unfamiliar. Michael didn't understand.

"What's your name?" The voice repeated.

Michael opened his eyes. He saw a strange form hovering over him. It was covered in a white, streaming glow. Was it a ghost? Angel? For some reason, he was afraid. He felt himself try to escape, but he couldn't move.

"What's your name?" The voice demanded again.

Perhaps he could trust the light. He felt himself speak his name. "Pruett."

"Okay, Pruett, hold on. We're almost there," the light said, but the words sounded far away.

And then everything fell into darkness again.

D awn couldn't remember how long she had been on the floor. She had never blacked out before. Instantly Michael's accident came back to her, and she found herself running to her car. Its wheels burned the pavement as she pressed on the gas and screeched into gear, racing down her driveway. Keeping one eye on the road, she frantically found "Keeks," an affectionate name for Michael's brother, Chris, in Saint Louis, on her phone's contact list.

After a short, frenzied conversation in which Dawn gave the little information she had, she texted both Matt Deehan and Christina Feuz. She had seen them only a few hours before at the church picnic. No doubt the two would meet her at the hospital.

Spontaneous words tumbled out of her mouth as she drove. "God, what are you doing? You *cannot* take him away from me now! You can't take this one too!" She drew the back of her hand across her face, drying it.

The crying is over, she informed herself. *That's it.*

Her mother…Dawn knew she had suppressed the memory that was eerily similar to this. How many phone calls from hospitals was she doomed to receive? Dawn had only been in her late twenties when her mother was in an accident and had to be put on life support. The time came when Dawn and her brothers had to make the impossible decision to take her off. Tears did nothing for her mother then; they'd do nothing for Michael now.

Swerving into a parking space near the entrance of Saint John's ER, she ran toward its double glass doors. An ambulance still sat outside, although its lights were off and it was silent. Whirling around to take in the scene around her, she noted several EMTs talking with the hospital staff. One young man, taller than six feet, seemed to be frowning as he reported information to a nurse.

Just then, another EMT, a shorter woman in her mid-fifties with cropped hair stepped out from the double doors.

Dawn felt her heart pounding heavily. At no one in particular, and unsure of what to do or whom to talk to, she asked loudly, "What's going on?"

"Ma'am," she heard the tall young man say.

She shifted her body to look up at him several feet away. His eyes held compassion, but before he could reach Dawn, a nurse grabbed her arm and started to walk her inside.

"Are you Mrs. Michael Pruett?" She asked kindly, taking in Dawn's outfit.

She'd had time to perfect her hair, makeup, and clothes while she had been waiting at home for Michael. The nurse's calm nature soothed her beating heart.

"Yes, I am. Please tell me what's happening."

```
┌─────────────────────────────┐
│     JULY 15, 2012           │
│  EMERGENCY ROOM, SAINT      │
│     JOHN'S HOSPITAL         │
│      17:43 MT               │
└─────────────────────────────┘
```

T rent noticed a petite woman with neatly curled, shoulder-length hair standing close by, listening to his conversation.

She must be the wife, he realized. For a moment Trent's breathing intensified. Seeing family members' reactions to their loved ones made his job more difficult. Strangely, she seemed in control of her emotions. *Thank God.*

He called out to her, and she suddenly steered toward him, but a nurse reached her first. "Mrs. Pruett…"

She turned to walk into the hospital alongside the nurse, unfaltering in her gaze. Trent could overhear her steady voice, "Tell me what's happening."

As the figures disappeared around a corner, he realized that was it. There was nothing else they could do, and there were no assurances. Michael might live and be facing the difficult recovery of a spine and head injury. Or, he could die. Either way, his wife would be left with the consequences.

Trent unconsciously fingered the cross underneath his paramedic garb again. He turned back to another nurse who had asked him a question and continued to rattle off information as if on autopilot. That part was easy. He could assess and diagnose the situation without effort.

Cori joined Trent as he was finishing, and when their eyes met, he shook his head in relief. Eleven minutes—that's all it had been. He looked down at his hands. They were shaking.

Cori reached up to pat his shoulder. "Time to go, Trent. It's over."

She was more practiced than he at letting go. She was forced to push through that sense of helplessness when she had watched a loved one slip away into death in front of her. Since then she had seen people die dozens of times.

They walked slowly back toward the ambulance, which now sat waiting in silence.

Brian followed behind and attempted to lighten the intensity by focusing on the next task at hand. "Rig clean up!"

Trent barely heard him. He peered down at his watch: 5:45. The patient was still within the golden hour—the first hour after the accident. It increased his chance of survival.

Trent knew what the man's quality of life was likely to be. He would be a paraplegic, confined to a wheelchair. He didn't know if he'd ever see Michael Pruett alive again. Sometimes families of emergency victims would find the team members and thank them, but sometimes they never heard how things turned out.

During his hours of training in Utah, priests would come alongside the ambulance to offer prayer. Praying couldn't hurt.

"God help him," he whispered under his breath. "Let him live."

The nurse placed her hand on Dawn's and directed her down the entryway of Saint John's. "Your husband has been in an accident. His motorcycle collided with a large truck downtown. Unfortunately, he didn't have his helmet on."

Dawn nodded her head. "He never wears his helmet in town."

The nurse continued. "Michael was dragged under the truck for quite a few feet. He has suffered a very severe head injury."

"Please," Dawn interrupted in a daze. She didn't know if she could handle knowing the details of his condition without hearing the prognosis. "Please…" She began again, more calmly. "I just want to know if he's going to be okay." She was surprised at the emotionlessness in her voice.

The nurse slowed outside the door of a room that Dawn assumed was Michael's. She appeared sympathetic, yet guarded. Dawn looked past her to peer through the blinds, but they were closed from the inside.

"Mrs. Pruett, at this point we simply can't say."

"Let me see him," Dawn stated flatly.

The nurse hesitated. "I need to prepare you for what you're going to see…"

Dawn stared at her, trying to be unshaken.

"Your husband's scalp was ripped open. A doctor is stapling it back in place as we speak, but he is conscious, which is a good sign."

"Conscious? He's awake?" Dawn felt like she might be sick again. The image of Michael lying there, fully aware of his head being stapled back together made her nauseous and light-headed.

The nurse finished talking as she opened the door to the room. "His upper body is unstable, and his ankle is also broken."

She excused herself as Dawn caught sight of Michael's bed. His head had swollen to nearly twice its size. His skull was exposed. Large gashes—apparent wounds from the staples that were holding his scalp together—were scattered across the top and left side of his head. His flesh was scarlet and still seething droplets of blood that gushed down to intermix with draping gauze. The doctor hadn't taken the time to shave him before stapling his scalp back on.

Dawn inhaled sharply and stood unmoving. She watched remotely. She couldn't find the courage to step past the doorframe. Michael lay on a board on top of a gurney. He hadn't been transferred to the bed, and his body thrashed unrestrained. The doctor stood by his bedside, a staple gun clutched in her right hand. Her gloves and even her scrubs were splotched with Michael's blood.

Suddenly Michael jerked and thrashed his body, tearing the IV from his arm. He winced in pain and cried out shocking, blatant profanities. The doctor reacted instantaneously and reattached the tube with prowess, ignoring the offensive words. She finally looked up from the disarray, greeted Dawn, and hurriedly exited the room.

Dawn was left standing alone, and she shuddered. She knew that Michael, a virile outdoorsman, hated to be confined, especially within the drab white walls of a medicinal-smelling hospital. His continuous incomprehensible phrases indicated that he didn't understand what had happened to him. His brain was attempting to compensate and make sense of the pain.

She felt a hand on her back. The simple act of care disturbed the heaviness that threatened to weigh her down. She turned to find Matthew Deehan. Although she had seen him only a few hours before, it felt like weeks ago now.

He placed his arm around her and pulled her to him.

Though she wouldn't admit it, she needed his reassuring touch. She held on to him, and together they walked toward Michael.

"Good God! What a bloody mess!" Deehan commented, referring to the staple gun that sat—with blood and hair still attached—on the shelf above Michael's head. He fully took in Michael's situation and moved toward the chairs that rested against the wall. "I need to sit down."

"Really?" Dawn shakily responded. "Less than one minute. Not your best time."

Deehan lowered his head and placed it between his hands. "Yeah," he answered in a weak attempt at wit. "I suppose that in this case you win."

"Your skin looks green."

He moaned and groped his mess of hair in angst. "Just give me a few."

"You're right though," she said as she looked over the scene. "It is a bloody mess." She breathed in deeply and reached out toward Michael, but she drew back after realizing that his body was situated too precariously to touch him.

"Michael, it's me," she began hesitantly.

"Dawn…" Michael choked out. His eyes were open, but unseeing.

"I'm here," She reassured him.

He calmed slightly, and disjointed words seethed out of his mouth, "Where...am...I? What...ha...happened?"

Dawn felt her hand squeeze into a fist. "You've been in an accident, Michael."

He spat out a series of unintelligible words.

"An accident. You've been in an accident," she repeated, hoping that Michael would understand if she simply clarified things. She wanted him to respond like normal. He was always so strong. Why couldn't he just sit up, wipe off the blood and bruises, and walk out of the room?

Michael didn't seem to hear her. "What's...happening to me? Why am I here?"

"Where are the nurses?" Dawn cringed in frustration. She felt useless against his severe pain. She turned to look at Deehan for help, biting her lip.

Deehan didn't move from his seat, but gave her a sympathetic half-smile in resignation.

Just then a blonde, shorthaired, middle-aged doctor wearing glasses entered the room. She seemed wary as she inspected them both, her jaw tight. She approached Dawn. "Mrs. Pruett." Her voice was direct, without warmth.

"Dawn."

"Dawn," she reiterated. "Michael has an obvious abrasion to his head. We don't know the extent of his other wounds, but we are concerned about head trauma, bleeding and hematoma of the brain."

"Brain trauma...hematoma?" Dawn echoed her words.

"Hematoma appears much like bruising, but it's actually blood spilling outside of blood vessels into the tissue or muscle of the brain. Michael might have hematomas outside of his skull and inside of his brain that we need to assess with serial CT scans. Our technician left for the day but is on her way back to the hospital now." She hesitated before gesturing to the paperwork on her clipboard, "We will need you to sign here. This effectively states that you release Saint John's from any liability if your husband dies in the process of his care here."

The words felt blunt and unfeeling, but Dawn couldn't deny the severity or danger of Michael's case. Although Jackson Hole dealt with all forms of accidents due to being a top winter sport destination, Saint John's had minimal equipment and facilities for advanced cases. They relied heavily on helicopters and hospitals in larger cities within a four to five hour range.

"I don't understand," Dawn stated curtly. "Why can't we just MEDEVAC him to get the care he might need?" she asked.

"We can't release him until we know the full diagnosis." The doctor's eyes were furtive, as if she were avoiding Dawn.

"Why is he allowed to just…shouldn't he be more secure?" Deehan finally stood up and joined her.

"Without knowing the extent of his injuries, we don't want to take any chances by moving him…" The doctor's voice trailed off.

"What do I do?" Dawn asked Deehan quietly, not knowing how to make the decision.

He grimaced. "It seems like it's his only chance. I'd sign it."

Dawn reluctantly picked up the pen and signed her name. "Michael's in pain. What are you going to do for him *now*?"

The doctor gave a small smile of reassurance. "We're doing

everything we can. We've already given him narcotics. Unfortunately, there's nothing we can do at the moment for his nerve pain. I'll leave you to it," she finished, glancing at Michael and withdrawing from the room.

Michael was still thrashing about in agitation. Every so often he cried out in pain and attempted to grab his left shoulder.

Deehan approached the bed and placed his hands on Michael's shoulder.

Michael's hand slapped at him, and he swore again.

"It's okay, buddy! We're here to help you." Deehan reassured him. Then he began to massage Michael's shoulder. "I've never heard him speak like that. He sounds like me in traffic."

At first Michael kept fighting Deehan's touch, his fist nearly catching his friend's abdomen.

Dawn caught the wry smile on Deehan's face. Michael was in fight-or-flight mode. Deehan massaged harder, and it seemed to relieve some of Michael's pain. He let out a sigh and stopped cursing, at least for a few minutes.

The sound of the door opening turned Dawn's attention away from Michael. Dan and Christina Feuz entered the room, Christina still toting her newborn. Behind them were Nathan and Richard.

Dawn suddenly felt a sense of awkwardness. She looked down at Michael's messy appearance, his bloody scalp, out of character agitation, and the mass of medical tubes. For people to see her husband in such a vulnerable and depleted state seemed like an unfair contrast to the usual confident man they all knew. Knowing the feeling was irrational, she pushed it away and embraced the sudden relief she felt for seeing familiar, caring faces—all there to support. She couldn't formulate the words to thank them, but she knew they understood.

As Dawn embraced Christina, she could feel her tears wetting her friend's auburn hair. The familiar scent of Christina's perfume momentarily soothed Dawn in the harsh setting of the sterile room.

Dawn pulled away to greet the others. She did not know Nathan, a newcomer to Jackson Hole, that well. She paused slightly before giving Richard a hug. Even before Richard joined Michael's real estate company months before, the two men's relationship had been tenuous and competitive to say the least. Dawn only knew Richard in that context and, again, felt uncomfortable. But in this moment she was grateful for his presence in the room, for his father-like strength.

"What can we do?" Christina asked.

Dawn felt some of the helplessness fade as she considered Christina's bright eyes. "Just…pray."

Dawn lost consciousness of how long they prayed. Little by little, she began to feel at peace. Somewhere in the back of her mind, she heard a whisper, *He's going to make it.* She wanted to trust it. She needed to trust it. But even with the peace that her husband might stay alive, there were other issues, other questions involved. Michael might live, but was the life they knew together over?

She watched her husband move, attempting to escape again. She stood up from her seat next to the head of Michael's bed to stretch and noticed Deehan leaning against the wall on the other side of the room. He was casually but intentionally distancing himself from the rest of the group.

As emotional fatigue threatened to take over, she trod over the cold, unattractive tiles toward Deehan. The hospital had grown quieter as the night continued, and it felt eerily calm. "You okay?" she asked. Deehan's face looked like he had broken into a cold sweat.

"Yeah," he offered.

Nathan, aware of Deehan's demeanor, changed the subject. "He seems to have calmed down quite a bit. I think it helps when he hears our voices."

"And our prayers," Dawn added.

"Yeah, well…" Deehan cut himself short.

Nathan interjected, "Doctors have a job to do, and they have to prepare us for the worst-case scenario, but I also know that God has a bigger agenda here. Michael survived an accident that should have killed him. That's a legitimate miracle. We need to keep thinking about that because our faith makes a difference."

Dawn wanted to believe Nathan's words, to hope against hope or at least against logic. She watched Deehan react. He had turned his face away in an effort to hide annoyance or frustration—she couldn't quite tell. Instead she looked toward Christina's hands that rested on Michael's chest.

Deehan ran his hands through his hair in seeming desperation, swirling back toward them. "Why did this happen in the first place? Why do *all* shitty things happen?"

The outburst stunned the group into silence. No one responded until apparently Deehan decided that he had become entirely too philosophical. "I guess I'm thinking too much."

Nathan encouraged him, "Despite the situation, God is good."

"What the *hell* does that even mean? Letting horrible things happen is good?" He stared Nathan down. "It doesn't matter anyway."

Dawn froze momentarily, suddenly realizing that Deehan was looking down at Michael, but he was seeing Kristen, his best friend who had been killed by a freak accident only a year before. Dawn's thoughts flashed to Michael's sister-in-law, Keek's wife. She had suffered from a stroke and became paralyzed on one side of her body, never fully recovering. *Her children…* Michael's nieces and nephews would never know their mother as she had been. Her mind turned to her own children and how her girls had given Michael so much trouble. The guilt would crush them.

Nathan continued, intercepting her thoughts, "We all get it, Deehan. Bad things happen. There's no way around it. I just refuse to believe God causes them."

Then why? Dawn asked internally, her frustration beginning to rise to the exterior. She couldn't allow herself to believe it was merely Michael's carelessness for not wearing his helmet.

By the time Michael was checked in after the rescue, the technician that administered the CT scan had gone over the Teton mountain pass for the night. Thankfully, the staff had been able to reach her just before going out of range and when she arrived back the hospital several hours later, the nurses finally came to wheel Michael away.

His pain and fear seemed to return at their touch, and he hurled out more curse words. When they returned him to the room a little while later, Dawn felt the shock of his injuries all over again. She watched as they pushed the bed into position and locked the wheels. Her husband seemed unrecognizable to her. She had rarely seen Michael uncollected or unsure of himself, let alone completely helpless and physically—perhaps even mentally—broken. From the first second of knowing him, Michael had always been one of the most confident men she had ever met—to a fault. In fact, her first impression of him had not been a great one.

Dawn moved to Jackson a few years earlier after a wealthy businessperson bought the bank she worked for in Green River, Wyoming. He built another branch in Jackson and offered her a managerial position. Having been divorced for several years, the opportunity represented a fresh start with potential for promotion. She and three miniature versions of herself—Jade, Paige, and Karsen—packed up and moved that summer.

They left the world they knew, family BBQs and Grandma's house being down the road, to build a new life in a small resort town where they were completely unknown. Things didn't go the way Dawn had hoped. Her girls disliked Jackson, not only because it was foreign and strange, but because it represented the reality that their parents would never get back together again.

Michael called her soon after her arrival at the prodding of a mutual friend. Jackson was small, and apparently her presence had already been noted. He left a message for her to connect with him if she were interested. It was communicated in such a confident tone that Dawn assumed she knew exactly the kind of man Michael was: superficial and slightly full of himself, like most single men in the social circles of Jackson.

Dawn never responded to Michael. She was in a committed relationship in the first place, and in the second, she simply didn't want to. She hadn't even given him a second thought until running into him at a typical wine and cheese fundraising event some time later. By that point her serious relationship had become an official engagement. They greeted each other somewhat coolly. She was not that impressed with Michael though his attitude and connections made it clear that he was successful and well respected. When he excused himself from their circle of conversation, Dawn didn't bat an eye.

It wasn't until Michael approached her during the winter months a year later that she began to see a different man than the person she thought she had figured out. Feeling alone and cheerless, she had hoped for a familiar face in the grand foyer of the White Buffalo Club, a high-end hotel in the heart of Jackson. Instead of braving the social scene downstairs, she admired the high wooden beams and stonework overhead.

It beautifully contrasted with the faux Italian walls and the plush, darkly stained leather armchairs that stood beside polished granite tables. Her gaze was interrupted by a man's voice: "Dawn, do you remember me?"

It was Michael. He stood next to her, his dark blonde hair tousled from the wind. His polite, sincere smile greeted her.

Dawn felt herself blush slightly. "Yes. Michael?"

"Who are you waiting for?"

"Well," she hesitated, glancing behind him at the entryway. Outside, flurries of snow swirled wildly in the wind. It looked like her friends weren't going to show. "I'm waiting for my friend Tina, and—"

"Oh, I know Tina," Michael interrupted. "She'll most likely already be downstairs." He held out his arm to lead her. "I'll take you down. If she isn't here, you can stay with my friends and me until she arrives."

Dawn inhaled in relief—although she didn't dare let him know. Surprisingly, she was glad to walk into a room on the arm of someone with the confidence and social standing she so often discredited as pretentious. When Michael commented on her missing engagement ring, she was taken aback.

"You know," he had begun, his pleasant grin widening, "I'm beginning to believe that this fiancé of yours in non-existent. Like Sasquatch."

Dawn smiled at the memory. She had been intrigued by his playfulness. She had taken Michael's arm to descend the stars, but she stopped midway after hearing his comment and began to laugh—a full, deep laugh. She looked up at him with a wry smile. "What do you mean, *Sasquatch?*" The engagement had broken off abruptly and painfully, and for someone to be so light and direct about the topic oddly made her feel safe and even comfortable.

"You know…Bigfoot."

"Yes, I know *who*. I don't know *why*."

"I just mean that you hear stories about him, you see signs that he may have been this place or that, but no one can prove they have actually seen him. I think you made it all up."

That comment won her over, although she did not know it at the time and could never explain why. Michael had become a real person, a real personality. They sat and talked during the whole event, and the more Michael joked and opened up to her about his family and work, the more she liked him. By the time the party was over, they had decided to head to the Cowboy Bar, a renowned tribute to the Wild West that featured dancing and live music. Dawn enjoyed those hours more than she had anticipated. Yet when Michael led her to the dance floor, she could sense herself holding back.

"Are you trying to lead or something?" Michael called out to her above the din. Before she had time to answer, he leaned in and whispered, "Just let me lead you."

This small act of moving closer had been the beginning of Dawn trusting him. Michael with all his charm and confidence was a man who could take care of himself, and because of that—Dawn figured—he might even be able to take care of her.

She longed to remain in those safe, warm memories. How could she make sense of reality? It was difficult to accept that the accident had really happened. Yes, things had been strained with Michael and her girls during their two years of marriage, but life with Michael had been an adventure. She wasn't ready for it to end.

The same shorthaired, wary doctor entered the room in a rush, her glasses glinting. Another staff member and a nurse followed behind her. She cleared her throat uncomfortably and glanced down at her clipboard before finally scanning the room to find Dawn.

Everyone in the room quieted, looking anxiously at the group of medical professionals.

"Mrs. Pruett," she began hesitantly. "This is the technician that performed the CT scan." She gestured to the woman standing beside her.

Dawn acknowledged them both, sighing in relief that she would finally get an answer. Her heart thumped rapidly against her chest as she tried to mentally prepare for the diagnosis. As if he knew her internal dilemma, Deehan placed his hand on her shoulder. She knew that Deehan needed Michael's miracle as much as she did for more than one reason. She was grateful for his friendship. Deehan would be there day and night without question.

The doctor continued, "As we stated before, we were concerned about the trauma to Michael's head. The scans show he has had obvious trauma to his skull, his brain is bleeding, and his spinal cord has nearly been severed."

Before Dawn had time to consider her words, she heard herself petition with authority, "He needs to go to Salt Lake City. There's a first class trauma center there."

"We don't have the capability to handle this here in Jackson," the doctor agreed. Then she adjusted her stance uncomfortably. "The problem is that given his current condition, he might not survive the transfer. You need to brace yourself for the possibility…"

Dawn heard shuffling feet and a few murmurs in the background, but she remained cold. What was this news? She had finally convinced herself, even believed, that Michael would be okay.

"If he does survive, he will be paralyzed from the neck down."

Dawn found herself muttering out loud in the following silence, "*If?*"

The doctor cleared her throat. "As a staff, we are conversing to determine the best course of action," she continued in a calm, monotonous tone.

Michael began to struggle and call out again. Dawn worried over his constant state of agitation. His obvious discomfort was difficult to witness, but more than that, she also feared the movements would cause further damage. She couldn't comprehend why nothing was being done about it.

"I don't understand," Dawn concluded as she shook her head, a defensive thrust in her tone. "He's been thrashing around now for hours."

Deehan cut in to finish, "Shouldn't he be restrained?"

The staff clearly knew what was happening and turned amongst themselves for a few moments, eventually ending their discussion.

Neither Dawn nor Deehan understood.

The doctor went on to explain, "We need to talk through possibilities and decide what is best for him according to hospital regulations."

Someone handed Dawn another clipboard with more paperwork. She felt blind and powerless as she signed the papers. The facts were still unclear. What was going to happen? She did not know what she could or couldn't do as a wife, what she was giving permission for, or if it would make a difference in the end. She felt the throbbing pain in her heart physically ascend up into her throat. Her mouth grew dry, and she found that she couldn't even speak.

It felt like midnight, but Dawn wasn't sure. The hospital was quiet save for the beeping sounds of Michael's monitors and the scuffle of nurses' scrubs every now and then as they passed by the open doorway.

She blinked incoherently before taking note of the room. A few heads nodded in sleep. She realized that Richard had disappeared. Then her gaze fixed on Deehan who stood across the bed from her.

His eyes met hers, and he walked over and quietly pulled up a chair next to her. "I wonder what he's thinking about all of this," he whispered.

"Hopefully nothing. I really hope he's just…dreaming."

Dawn felt him watch her thoughtfully. "You should go outside of the room for a bit. I'll stay here with Michael. Go. Get coffee."

"I don't know. What if something happens and I'm not here?"

"Go on, get," Deehan prodded. "I will find you and bring you back. I promise."

Though Dawn felt uneasy, she sighed in relief as she left the room. Deehan was right. She needed a breather. She needed a change of scenery. She desperately needed coffee. She wandered the hallways before finding the cafeteria, which to her surprise was not empty. A few of the hospital staff were on break and laughing together in the middle of the room.

A family of four was sitting at one corner table; they all bore the same weariness in their eyes as she knew was in hers.

She retrieved a cup of coffee, but tried not to smell it. *Stale coffee. Not Starbucks.* She poured a drop of milk into the cup to make it bearable and turned toward the cash register. Richard stood in line in front of her.

This should be interesting, she thought, and from the expression on Richard's face, Dawn knew he probably felt the same.

"What are you still doing here? I mean, you…" Dawn said, interrupting herself, "I mean, it's kind of you to stay."

Richard breathed out a soft laugh. "I want to be here. How are you holding up?"

Dawn was tired of the question. Did it matter how she felt? Wasn't it obvious?

"I'm fine, I guess," she answered flatly.

"Yeah. The question doesn't need to be asked. I'm sorry," Richard said, reading her mind or perhaps her countenance.

For a second Dawn feared she had accidentally stated her thoughts out loud. "No. Forgive me, I'm exhausted."

"I'm sure. Do you want to sit down?" Richard asked, pointing toward a corner table nearby. "I'm getting some coffee," he continued. "I'll pay for yours too."

"No, please—" Dawn always felt uncomfortable when someone offered to help.

"Really. Let me." Richard turned to the woman at the register. "Two coffees," he said, handing her a wad of dollar bills from his wallet.

For the first few minutes at the table, Dawn and Richard made polite small talk. Dawn knew more about Richard from what Michael told her than she did from personal experience. The word *cutthroat* was often used. *What would Michael think of this*? She wondered, forcing a smile. The man seated across from her seemed gentle, harmless. Perhaps it was nothing more complicated than male competition.

"I know he'll pull through this," Richard said, reassuringly.

"Yes," Dawn agreed, her stomach cringing.

Richard gave her a sympathetic nod and turned his gaze to the black liquid filling his cup.

"All the way—I have no doubt. Michael is…" Richard searched for the word, and for the first time Dawn could see he was trying to find something nice to say about his business rival.

"What?" she asked, her defenses up, surprising them both.

"A fighter," Richard finished, grinning.

Dawn returned the expression. She knew the story. Things got ugly with both wrangling for clientele and outbidding each other.

"Yes, he is," Dawn said, sipping the last of her coffee. "I believe he'll survive. Maybe he'll even walk again someday. Even if he does, even if he can eventually take care of himself, he'll still lose everything." Dawn's thoughts were spiraling down. She couldn't catch her breath. "He might not be able to work again…his business—"

Richard studied her face without a word. Suddenly, Dawn felt insecure, sharing so much with a man she barely knew. Her lack of sleep was showing itself. What if Richard saw this whole accident as a chance for self-advancement?

"I'll see what I can do," Richard remarked calmly.

Dawn sensed his earnest interest, but how could he help, really?

"Thank you," she sighed, almost breathlessly. "I'd better get back up there in case something's happened. Thanks for listening." She stood up and pushed her chair under the table. "And for the coffee too, Richard," she added gratefully before turning away.

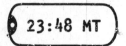

B y the time Dawn returned to Michael's room, everyone else had woken up. She headed over to the bedside, relieved that she hadn't missed anything.

Deehan was in the middle of a conversation with Somers. Glancing over her shoulder, she saw that she had come back just before a nurse shuffled through the door.

Deehan nodded at Dawn as if to say, *See? I told you I'd take care of everything.*

The nurse, tired and unfriendly, reported emotionlessly, "The Department of Neurosurgery at the University of Utah in Salt Lake City has agreed to accept him."

"Thank God!" Dawn declared, a smile expanding on her face.

Deehan exhaled noticeably and stretched his arms overhead. The others clapped and laughed as tension lowered in the room. Everyone forgot the nurse was still in the room until she continued talking, "A MEDEVAC Team will escort him from here to Salt Lake by helicopter. They'll work hard to make sure he survives the transfer, and Salt Lake will take it from there. It's one of the best neurosurgery centers in the nation."

Dawn had waited for so long to hear comforting news. *The best...*

Her eyes quickly locked on Deehan. "My girls. I need to tell the girls, and I don't know how."

He gazed down at her and added, "You probably need to call Michael's family again too...Keeks and Michelle."

"Oh God," Dawn answered quietly. "What do I say?"

"What can you say? The situation is still unknown at this point."

Giving Deehan an unappreciative look, she grabbed her phone from inside her purse.

"Did that answer your question?" She heard Deehan call behind her as she stepped out into the hallway and dialed Paige's number again.

"Mom, what happened? You okay?" Paige sounded unsure, her voice quieter than usual.

"Michael's been in an accident. I'm...not...I'm fine, I guess. As much as I can be anyway," Dawn stammered.

She knew Paige was gearing up to take charge. "So what do we need to do?"

"They are transferring his body—" Dawn caught herself. "Michael, I mean. They are taking Michael to Salt Lake. Deehan will come get you tonight on his way."

"Okay, I'll tell Jade and Karsen. What time should we be ready?"

"Honestly, I don't know. Definitely after four or five. Probably early morning."

Once Dawn finished talking with her daughter, she found herself dialing Keeks, Michael's brother, again. When he picked up, she could tell from his muffled voice that he had been crying.

"We've been searching for flights to Jackson all night. There's nothing. The only place we can get to is Salt Lake City."

"That's why I'm calling. They're actually moving him to Salt Lake," Dawn affirmed.

"Thank God!" He exclaimed gratefully. "We'll be there as soon as we can."

Dawn sighed in relief and reentered Michael's room. By this time, most of her friends were taking coffee or bathroom breaks. She and Deehan were left alone. She caught a glimpse of him resting his forehead on the side railing of Michael's bed before he noticed her and quickly sat up.

"It's okay," she affirmed. "You can have a minute alone if you want."

"I don't," Deehan returned crisply.

"I know this is hard for you, Deehan."

"For *me*? You're amazing."

"What do you mean?"

"I mean, I'm not the only one in this room in pain."

"I know," Dawn said, looking at Michael. "I can't imagine what it feels like to be…completely broken."

"Yes," Deehan agreed, "but I was talking about you."

For a brief moment, they stared at one another, exhausted.

Dawn felt worn to the bone, but she also knew it was moments like these that revealed the level of her strength. She realized at an early age that there were two types of people in life: those who allowed tragedy to define them and those who overcame it, learned from it, and became stronger because of it. Everything about her childhood could have given her a shadow to outrun the rest of her life, but Dawn refused to feel sorry for herself. In some ways, suffering made her a deeper person, wise to reality. She would rather that than the illusion of a perfect life.

Dawn took a seat and pulled her chair closer to Michael. "We argued about whether we were going to go out or stay in tonight—I mean last night. I wanted to stay in," she said, taking Michael's hand and studying his palm, his fingers. His hands were the least altered part of her husband's body.

"Looks like he won," Deehan said with a grin.

Dawn blushed, remembering she was still overdressed. "Yes. What's new?"

"He usually gets what he wants. Well…" Deehan looked at Michael's mangled body and caught himself. "Maybe not all the time."

Dawn considered the irony of Deehan's comment. Michael liked to get what he wanted and this obviously wasn't it. He liked to close deals, make money, be independent and active. She knew he wouldn't be doing any of what he wanted for quite some time.

"I remember when he called me a few months after we starting seeing each other. He'd been gone for a few days and couldn't believe I went out on a date with someone else. He's always been certain about things; he almost can't believe it when something doesn't happen the way he thinks it should."

She paused reflectively before adding, "He sounded like a disappointed father. He said that he didn't want to see other people and that he didn't want me to see other people. He told me the choice was mine, now that I knew where he stood."

She had never felt so frustrated and flattered at the same time. Who was this man, demanding that she make a choice? But it worked. She called him a few days after that phone call to let him know.

The MEDEVAC team interrupted Dawn's reverie. She didn't

recognize any of them. The six forms wore gray nylon pants and yellow jackets, and one already donned a white safety helmet. The lead paramedic, this time a female, stated brazenly, "Clear the room, please."

23:51 MT

"Keeks, Michelle!" Michael heard his siblings' names being called. He wanted to see them, but he was surrounded by darkness. He could hear his sister laughing. Suddenly, she appeared before him as a teenager, her cheeks bright, the sun hot overhead.

"Happy Fourth!" she said. *Where were they?*

Then Michael saw Keeks with an armful of t-shirts standing under the Saint Louis Arch. "Sweet t-shirts for twenty bucks!"

Michael remembered…Keeks had designed t-shirts and they were selling them. They had worked so diligently. The comforting scene didn't stay. It grew faint and became smaller as if Michael were being pulled far away. Flashes of other scenes from high school appeared—leading his football team as the quarterback, parking cars, mowing lawns. Always saving money. Always running toward something greater.

"Son!" It was his father's voice again. The tone was affectionate and carried unusual gusto.

Michael heard himself tell his father. "$25,000 a year, Dad. Isn't that great?" His memories were becoming clearer. He recollected that conversation on the phone. *My first job. A business consultant.*

"And, Dad…" he hesitated.

"Yes, Son?"

"I'm going to ask Rachel to marry me."

His father never answered.

Instantaneously Michael felt pain throughout his body. Why was Rachel associated with pain? He hadn't seen her in a very long time... *Why?* Suddenly he was standing outside of their apartment. He tried to open the door, but it was locked. He couldn't find the key. *Did I ever have it?* His thoughts felt heavy, weighed down by disappointment. *Why won't Rachel let me in?*

His father's words called to him again, attempting to rescue him. "You can do anything you want in life, Son."

Somewhere, at some point, Michael knew he had been successful. Business had been lucrative. Hadn't he done everything right? Was he still successful?

"No," Michael heard himself say. He shook his head. "That's not true, Dad. I tried. I tried, and I failed." He wanted to walk away, to leave and never look back, but there wasn't a door. There wasn't even a window.

His father's voice evaporated. Instead, he heard the echo of his own failure. Suddenly he was laying flat on a table in a morgue, his body pale and bruised. He was being eaten alive from the inside out—rotting slowly away like he was made of infectious cells. He tried to scream, but there was only silence. He realized he had been eroding for some time. The disease, the pain, seemed to be mocking him, telling him that he was already dead. He tried to move, to sit up and prove it wrong, but he couldn't.

How did this happen?

And then Michael knew—the pain was going to kill him.

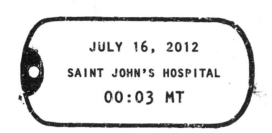

They watched the MEDEVAC team together through the open door. Michael had grown calm earlier, but now, sensing movement and strangers around him, he began to writhe and call out, "What's happening? Get your damn hands off me! I want out! Do you hear me?" He jerked the IV out of his left arm again.

The paramedic that had been leaning over him jumped aside to avoid being assaulted.

Dawn cringed at Michael's untamed reaction. *That is not my husband...* She watched as they prepared to move his defensive body. The paramedic gripped the C-collar attached to his neck.

Michael cursed at her.

Several others grabbed the board below him on either side, while still another held the prepped gurney in place.

"On my lead," the woman at Michael's head stated curtly. "One, two, three."

Within seconds they had lifted the board that held Michael and set it on the waiting gurney. Though they used force to make his body cooperate, they strapped him down with ease and precision. The strappings looked similar to those of a psychotic patient.

At least he's not capable of hurting himself anymore, Dawn thought.

As the team began to wheel him out of the room and into the hallway feet first, Dawn suddenly realized that they weren't going to take her with them. She grabbed the paramedic's arm. "Please, I want to go with my husband!"

The woman stopped, and turned to look at her gently. "Ma'am, there's only so much weight allotment on the helicopter. We simply can't allow family to travel and put the copter at risk." She gave Dawn a cursory glance and then a furtive smile. "I know you are small, but we can't make an exception. No one else on board. Rules are rules."

"Forget the rules!" Dawn answered. "If he doesn't make it, this will be my last time to see him alive." She felt the barricaded tears crash through again.

"I'm sorry," she heard the paramedic say, but she didn't accept her plea. Dawn's hand grew limp as she removed it from the woman's arm.

The paramedic continued to look at Dawn sympathetically, "We'll take care of your husband, Ma'am. You can walk with us to the roof if you'd like."

When Dawn finally released a weak smile, the paramedic gave her a reassuring nod. As Dawn plodded slowly behind the team, Christina embraced her.

They wheeled Michael away quickly. His tormented voice became softer, and his restricted movements less noticeable as his body became smaller and smaller. When the team reached the service elevator, they disappeared from sight.

This is it, Dawn thought. *This determines everything.*

Deehan came up beside Dawn and Christina, ushering them on. Nathan followed them, and Richard stayed behind.

They trudged silently down the empty hallway, entered the waiting guest elevator one-by-one, and huddled together until the bell dinged through the silence when they arrived at the roof. The group exited to a night sky looming bright overhead and sheltered their bodies from large gusts of wind coming from the helicopter's rotating blades. The massive yellow structure, edged in bright red, was large enough to seat the entire emergency team.

Dawn could no longer hear anyone's voice over the loud whine. The medics lifted the gurney inside and closed the cabin door without glancing their way.

"Please," Dawn urged unconsciously.

As if in response to her, the paramedic turned from the cockpit and gave her a final wave. The skids lifted off the ground, and the wind became more furious.

She squinted against the wind as her husband traveled away from her, perhaps for the last time. Nothing else in Dawn's entire life could compare to that sense of loss.

Deehan grabbed her arm. "Dawn."

She looked up at him through her tears.

"Let's go. Let's get your girls."

G reen River, Wyoming was a four-hour drive from Jackson Hole. The plan was to pick up the girls from their father's house in the early morning hours and then drive on separately to Salt Lake City—hopefully— by the time the sun rose. Under any other circumstance, the spontaneity of the night would have suited Deehan just fine. Impulsiveness energized him, the surprisingly meaningful conversations, last-minute detours, and midnight exploits. In fact, this was what drew Michael to him and him to Michael. Both loved to be out and about in the world, often hiking, hunting, and trekking through snow together in silent woods. Deehan always considered himself more calibrated for that lifestyle than Michael, who seemed to enjoy adventure within the structure of stability. Deehan, on the other hand, welcomed the unknown.

Dawn talked around their reason for the drive, and Deehan let her. His laid back, playful attitude put people at ease, and he was happy to relieve her mind of contemplating the future at least for a couple of hours. All welcomed his accent and mannerisms, and he was often described—by himself and others—as "a strapping young lad." This confidence and appeal proved to be quite useful, especially in Jackson's society.

Soon, they stopped at a gas station to fill up. Deehan bought chewing tobacco and peered down the aisle at Dawn, who was perusing the candy section and holding a bag of beef jerky. For a split second he forgot that this wasn't a pit stop on a normal road trip.

When Dawn caught him with a sly look, she remarked, "Aren't we a sight?"

"I don't know, I gotta look better than that jerky." He leaned heavily on the vowels for a full Massachusetts effect.

Dawn laughed, her face beaming with appreciation for his humor.

Deehan congratulated himself. This was the Dawn he knew.

For the first few minutes back on the road, both were quiet. Deehan turned the radio on, but after scanning through what seemed like countless commercials and muffled country music, he turned it off.

They sat in silence.

Suddenly, he started to chuckle. He could never be completely serious without an effort to lighten the mood.

"What? *What* are you possibly thinking right now?" Dawn demanded.

"I was just thinking that when Michael comes out of this, he'll have a great excuse for everything. He already got lost all the time anyway. Now he can just say, 'I got hit by a truck and they stapled my head together, what do you expect from me?'"

The moonlight seeped through the window, illuminating Dawn's face, which appeared lighter with her laughter. "Yeah, sometimes it was like he was already out of it anyway. Like when he took us camping and forgot the tent…"

"Right?" Deehan said, visually noting her relief.

"We got to the camping spot on the river, and Michael started bellowing out orders to my girls to gather their gear and start setting up camp. So I asked him what I could do, and Michael yelled back, 'Look for the blue bag.' But I couldn't find it. So, I said, 'Um, there is no blue bag….'"

"'What? Dammit!' Michael said. 'That's our tent!' You should have seen the color drain from his face! He kept saying he was sorry and that he was such an idiot."

Deehan laughed. That was Michael, all right.

"I asked him why it was such a big deal. It bothered him a lot that he forgot it. He kept questioning how he was ever going to be able to take care of my girls and me if he couldn't remember a tent on a camping trip. I don't know…it seems like if he can't do things the 'right' way, he just beats himself up about it."

Deehan agreed. "Michael still doesn't know how to feel okay when life throws him curve balls, when he can't control an outcome…when things don't go as planned."

But Deehan didn't want to dwell on any lessons Michael needed to learn. What was the point now? His mind returned to the moment he first saw Michael's body at Saint John's, the shock of seeing his friend's familiar face covered in bruises, his scalp stapled back on his head. He shook his head to displace the memory. "Remember when Somers and I bought him a GPS to take on one of our hunting trips? He took it with him into the trees and came back several hours late because he somehow managed to lose it in the brush. The guy got lost trying to find the GPS device! I mean, seriously, the man can't be helped." Deehan loved Michael like a brother, and teasing his brother was one of his favorite pastimes. Banter was a type of love language for him, and Dawn was a good match for him any day, especially where her husband was concerned. The two could swap stories about Michael's mishaps for hours.

"It is so true," Dawn belted out. "He's either going to be worse than before or somehow have a new superpower. Like an internal mapping system."

"And then there was the time we went on a fishing trip and Michael forgot his fishing rod."

Dawn's smile faded.

Deehan noted her changed demeanor and decided it was best to let her do most of the talking.

Finally, Dawn said what was on his mind. "I think it's just nice to forget how serious it is. I keep going between hope that God will hear me and all of our prayers, and the grim reality of the situation that he might survive but need a caretaker for the next forty years."

The idea quieted Deehan. The thought of an outgoing Michael being confined to an indoor existence was too much to consider. "You don't have to go there if you don't want to," he said, attempting to remain calm. "Anyway, I don't think I'm the one to give any answers. My prayers get lost somewhere between my mouth and the ceiling."

"Why would you think that?" Dawn asked quietly.

"I don't have that great of a track record."

"You mean with…" Dawn hesitated.

"Kristen. Yes."

"I don't see why that means God doesn't hear you. Many people were praying."

"Yes," Deehan stammered. "I get that. But I wasn't just praying or asking God to heal her."

"What do you mean?"

"I begged God with my own life for Kristen to survive. Not just for me but for her little girl," he choked out. "She was basically an angel, and I'm not just saying that because I loved her. Kristen was literally the kindest person. The world needs kind people, but somehow they end up in accidents while crazy, racist dictators live to be a hundred and twenty. There's no answer for it. I'm not even sure I know what the question is." Deehan shook his head at his sentimentality, which was usually hidden behind his brazen demeanor.

"I don't know either," Dawn offered. "All I know is that Michael is the reason I even believe God cares about me. I can't imagine that Michael would want either of us to get angry at God and stop believing when he spent his whole life wanting others to see how much God loves them."

"Yeah, but that's what makes me sick," Deehan said, his voice raised and blunt. "He has spent his whole life believing, and now he is critically injured, possibly crippled forever, lying helpless in a hospital bed. I don't know what to do with that."

"You can't do anything. I think we have to—I know I have to—just see this thing through. I can't shake the feeling that there's still hope as long as he is alive. I have to believe…" Dawn put her hands over her face and began to sob uncontrollably.

Deehan unconsciously gripped the steering wheel more tightly. He had already suffered a huge loss, and now Michael might be gone too. The pain of losing Kristen had left a void inside that he had not and probably would never be able to fill. What was the point in believing in God if it didn't change anything? This was the time to reach over and comfort Dawn, yet he couldn't.

Sometimes the memories came in sudden spurts. He would be in the middle of a conversation or waiting in line at the post office, and then suddenly, as if transported, he would be alone in Kristen's hospital room, kneeling beside her, praying.

It had taken him three attempts to enter her room. He had turned around the first two times, uttering, "Holy shit." When he was finally able to walk toward her maimed body, he kept his eyes lowered. He desperately wanted to look into her eyes, but he couldn't. Instead, after kneeling on the floor, he ran his hand up the railing of the bed and searched blindly for her hand to hold it. Then, he gathered the courage to look at her hand. It was clean. No blood. No mess. That's all he needed. Her hands and feet were the only parts of her body that remained untouched.

He pleaded with her, "Everyone is begging for you to fight, Kristen, to fight for your life. But that's not what I'm going to ask you. I can't be selfish. It's your decision. And if you decide to go...we're all going to be okay." He remembered his final words to God about her, *I just ask that if she goes, You take her quickly.*

And she went quickly.

He could still remember the sound of Kristen's heart monitor flat lining, the rush of nurses into the room.

Deehan was brought back into the present by a stinging sensation in his hands. He looked down to see that his knuckles had turned white, and he loosened his grip around the steering wheel.

Dawn continued to relieve her anxiety through tears. "I have to get this out before I see the girls. I can't let them see me like this."

If only he could swap places with Michael, perhaps Dawn wouldn't go through the same pain he had. *I would much rather be the victim.* "Look," he said, trying to reassure them both. "It's different with Michael. After the collision, Kristen's brain never showed any sign that it was functional. It was like she died the instant of the accident even though her body was still physically alive. Michael has shown every sign that his brain is okay. Kristen died the next day. Michael could make it and be completely fine once he recovers."

"I know," Dawn mumbled. Then she suddenly gasped and slowly turned to look at him. "Oh my God!"

Reacting, Deehan swerved then shot a glance at Dawn, "What!?"

"Michael knew this would happen," she stated bluntly.

"Okay. Um, explain please."

"Michael sent me an email earlier this summer. And…"

"*And?*" Deehan prompted again.

"And I remember he said something like, 'Dawn, you are usually the one who senses spiritual things. I don't understand why I feel this way or what's coming, but I know that together we will be facing some very difficult times. We will be tested in our marriage. You know I love you, and you know that I'll stand by you until the end.'"

Deehan glanced sideways to gauge her reaction. She seemed to be in shock, transfixed on the memory.

The end of what? Deehan wondered. "He's going to pull through, Dawn," he stated forcefully, attempting to break her flashback.

"*Why?*" Dawn asked quietly.

"Why what?"

"Why would Michael feel like something bad was coming before it happened?" Dawn murmured, turning to look out her passenger window.

Deehan wanted to say something, anything. "Maybe it was God's way of preparing you." He barely believed his own words.

"I should have known, I should have—" she added, oblivious to his words.

"Dawn," Deehan spoke loudly. "Look at me."

When she shifted toward him, her eyes remained lowered for a few more seconds before finally staring upward into his.

Deehan gritted his teeth. "Michael has experienced a lot of miracles so far, right?"

"Right," she choked out, wiping tears off her cheeks.

"Right," he repeated. "I mean, think about it. You are on sabbatical—a sabbatical that your boss gave you without asking. That's a pretty darn obvious *coincidence*." His words sounded more courageous than he felt.

"Maybe God's grace looks like preparing you for what is to come. He's giving you a promise so that you can make it through without despairing." Deehan shook his head, the muscles in his cheek twitching. The thought made him remember his own premonition.

"You know what's weird? I had just been thinking about Kristen when you texted me about Michael. What's even weirder is that I was passing by the site of her accident at that moment. It was…perfect timing," he said, an undertone of anger and pain beginning to surface, "or not."

"I'm sorry Kristen didn't survive. I'm sorry for her family. For you. For her missing out on her child's life. I just don't understand it," Dawn added.

Deehan wondered what there was to understand. Life is life, and death is a part of it. At least that was the simple, realistic answer he had used to bury his own questions. But these weren't the words to share with Dawn, not now. "When she died, I thought I'd lost everything. She was... my best friend. We could never quite make sense of our relationship, so when she got married, I thought I'd lost her then. But just knowing she was happy was enough to make me happy. Now when I see her husband with her little girl, there is an actual void there. I see it in them. I feel it in me."

Dawn understood. "If I lose Michael, I'll lose everything. There's no one outside of Michael that knows me that well."

Dawn's cell phone rang suddenly. Aroused from her late night stupor, she groped to pick it up. Deehan noticed that her hands were trembling as she pushed the speakerphone button.

"Hello?"

"Mrs. Michael Pruett?"

She breathlessly released the response, "Yes."

"I'm glad we reached you. This is the Emergency Room at the University of Utah, and I'm calling to let you know your husband arrived. He is safe in our care now."

"Thank you!" She looked over at Deehan, who grinned approvingly.

"Can you tell me anything else?"

"That's all we can disclose at this time. We'll fill you in more when you arrive."

The line went dead.

"He made it," she stated emotionlessly. She was empty, drained.

Deehan shook his head. "As much as I hate to say it, I can't believe it. Something so much bigger is going on here."

Dawn exhaled loudly and set down the phone. She shifted in her seat and cracked opened the window to let in the fresh night air.

Deehan looked down at his fists that were still clenched around the wheel. He started slowly, "I have another chance, Dawn."

"What do you mean?"

"I have another chance to be there with my best friend and will, hopefully, see him survive. I will stay by your side and do whatever it takes—even quit my job if I have to—to be there for you guys. Second chances don't come often."

Deehan peered at the long stretch of road ahead of them. The moon's slivered shape peeked through the top part of the windshield. He looked up at it, remembering how many times he and Kristen had gazed at that moon, the sky, the mountains together. Why hadn't God saved her?

"You should lie back and try to sleep for a little bit," he advised. "I'll wake you when we get closer to Green River."

"The girls will be exhausted when we pick them up," Dawn said, lowering her seat.

"You can all take turns driving once you switch cars, and the others can sleep in the back," Deehan added. "Everyone will get a chance to rest."

Dawn nodded and closed her eyes.

"Everyone but poor Deehan, that is," he said in a mock whine. When he turned toward Dawn, he noted with content that she was already asleep.

D awn and the girls were directed to Michael's room after arriving at the Salt Lake hospital. Paige, being the most openly affectionate daughter, wrapped her arms around her younger sister, Karsen, as they walked down the long bare hallways. The oldest and most introverted of the three, Jade, ambled on beside them, lost in thought. The halls were dismally lit and nearly noiseless at that early hour except for the sound of their shoes squeaking on the lime green tiles.

Abruptly, Dawn's phone rang. It was Deehan.

"Hey, I'm lost," he stated curtly. The gruff voice revealed a lack of sleep and apparently, a foggy sense of direction. Once they had arrived in Green River, Dawn and the girls had continued on in a separate car, leaving Deehan on a solo mission. "I'm at a place called 'Uncle Jack's Crab Shack.'"

Dawn stopped walking momentarily and snickered, "Uncle Jack's

Crap Shack? Wait, *what*?" Realizing her mistake, she spouted out directions; he was only fifteen minutes away.

"All right," Deehan stated more light-heartedly than before. "I'll meet you at his room."

The drive from Green River to Salt Lake had been gruesome. Dawn sat in the front while Paige, her middle child, drove. Being practical and positive like her mother, Paige did her best to encourage everyone, but no one was calm. In the rear seat, Karsen had lain her head on Jade's lap and fallen asleep right away. Jade's hair created a dark curtain above her sister so that she could remain safely alone.

As much as Dawn longed to be strong for them and not break down, when she wasn't dozing in and out of sleep, she was crying. The girls didn't quite know what to think of this. Their mother rarely cried and kept emotions to a minimum. They were all scared, and the feeling was palpable.

Paige prompted her mother with more cheerful thoughts, "Mom, remember that time when we went…"

Dawn would oblige her with a nod or half-hearted response, although in her mind, she was busy coaxing herself to believe that Michael would somehow make it through. She pictured her strong husband pedaling his mountain bike down a rocky path and posing for a photo at the lake. Then one of the girls' faces would float into view and Dawn wondered how they would react to the worst-case scenario. They didn't share her faith. Would they ever get a chance to see Michael as he really was, a man who had given so much of his time and support from the beginning of their relationship? Despite her fear, Dawn still believed Michael would somehow make it through or at the very least, God would get her through this.

Now walking with her girls down yet another hospital hallway, Dawn became eerily calm, as if she had cried out every drop of sadness, draining her well of emotion. When they neared the waiting room, her pace softened, and she could feel her presence slow down like a steady heartbeat.

Jade glanced at her questioningly. "Mom?" Three sets of big azure eyes surveyed her closely.

She looked at her daughters thoughtfully. "I can't explain it, but I know that he's going to be okay."

"I'm glad you think so, Mom. I'm glad for that." Jade expressed what the other two girls didn't have the strength to say. With Paige and Karsen following suit, the group arrived in the ICU with a collective calm that was almost unnatural. The nurse met them at Michael's door where they could hear him cursing at the top of his lungs and an equally obnoxious monitor beeping in the background. The sounds brought back the all too familiar memories of Saint John's Hospital, and Dawn hesitated.

"Mrs. Pruett?" The nurse asked in a friendly manner.

She nodded.

The nurse introduced herself as "Paula" and escorted the family inside the room.

When Dawn registered the overwhelming amount of medical gear attached to her husband's body, she vacillated near the doorway in astonishment.

Somewhere between the rhythmic beats of the monitor, she heard her phone ring again. She looked over protectively at the girls. Her girls were frozen, immobilized by the sight of Michael's injuries and the maze of tubes and cords protruding from his body. Gasping lightly, Paige and

Karsen held back tears while Jade gathered every ounce of inner strength to appear unflustered.

Dawn didn't want them to see their stepfather this way.

"Mom!" Paige exclaimed.

Dawn's thoughts continued. She knew that Jade felt a lot more than she expressed. She was like her mother in that way, and being the oldest, Jade led by example. The monstrosity of machines and mangled skin was overwhelming. Dawn felt helpless to comfort them.

"Mom! Your phone is ringing," Paige said, grasping her wrist.

Dawn glanced down at her phone, still in a stupor. It was Deehan again. As she slowly raised the phone, she breathed out, "Deehan." She hoped he would make some snide remark to take her out of the nightmarish scene.

"So, I'm on the first floor at the reception desk, but the ladies here can't find Michael's room."

"Oh," Dawn answered. "Nancy Kelp."

"What?" Deehan asked, confused.

"Yeah, his name is Nancy Kelp," She said, feeling her voice grow stronger. "Since he's in the ICU, his real name is protected."

"Nancy Kelp," Deehan repeated. Then he chortled. "They gave him a woman's name? *Naaancy.*" He exaggerated the vowel sound in mock southern drawl.

Dawn exhaled and attempted a smile.

"I'm sorry. I'm looking for Nancy Kelp, not Michael Pruett. I get them confused all the time," she heard him jest in the background. "All right. Be right up," he told her.

With more focused strength, Dawn turned back to Michael's broken form and stepped nearer. The black, blue, and red trauma marks stretching across his body were more clearly evident now that time had passed. He had a cast on his left leg to mend his broken ankle.

"Go ahead," Paula encouraged.

Dawn had forgotten that she and the girls were not alone.

"Let him know you're here. He's semi-cognizant," she continued.

Dawn took a deep breath and walked up next to Michael, touching the bedframe. "Michael, I'm here. The girls are here with me."

Michael couldn't move his head, but his eyes darted toward Dawn. He seemed calm for a moment as if he understood, but then he began to flail his arms and legs and called out in a booming voice, "Help me! Get me out of here! These people are keeping me prisoner!"

His pleas were almost too much, but Dawn had to remain strong for him. She glanced at her youngest girl, Karsen. She didn't know what to say about his condition.

Paula, ignoring Michael's plea for help, pointed out the halo-type crown that had been screwed into the top of his head. Spewing from the crown were several cords that looked like strings. Attached to the strings and lying on the floor below the top of his bed were free weights.

"Michael's spinal column has been separated, and the spinal cord is stretched out over the separated spine," she explained. "We're hoping to cause the spine and spinal cord to straighten out by attaching weights to the cords hanging from his head."

Dawn nodded, attempting to register what was happening as well as what was being said, but the archaic pulley system was such a surreal apparatus that Paula's voice droned into a dull buzz.

Just then, Deehan entered the room, took one look at Michael, and spoke the words Dawn had failed to formulate. "What the *hell*? What kind of medical treatment is this?"

Evidently good-natured, Paula laughed as she ducked a swing by one of Michael's fists. She quickly maneuvered around the bed and adjusted a tube that had jostled lose from its perch nearby.

"Good Lord!" Dawn finally expressed. "I'm sorry. I don't know why he's acting like that!"

"Oh, it's normal for patients that have experienced brain trauma to be aggressive," Paula answered nonchalantly. "He is not himself right now, and no one is judging him for it. He is fighting for his life."

"He seems normal to me," Paige said, trying to break the tension with a touch of derision. But only Deehan chuckled as she made her way across the room and sat in one of the extra chairs by the window.

As Deehan walked toward the top of Michael's bed to peek at the strings and weights, the nurse went on, "This is what we call 'traction.' Eighty pounds of weight are on those strings. He's been on it for a few hours now. We'll give him about twelve hours to see if it makes a difference."

"Um, okay. I guess this is what we call 'modern medicine,'" Deehan blurted out obtrusively. "I could've rigged this up in my garage."

Michael thrashed toward Deehan and cursed vehemently. Unfazed by Deehan's sarcasm and Michael's outbursts, Paula continued. "You know, when we first saw the CT scans sent over by Jackson Hole, we expected a paraplegic."

Dawn and Deehan were mute for a moment, their glazed eyes exchanging a separate conversation.

"So, what are you saying?" Deehan prodded.

"Well, it's like something…*special* is going on here." Paula, becoming hesitant, excused herself and walked out of the room.

Deehan pushed his hands through the dark waves of his hair in obvious frustration and walked over to place his arm around Dawn. "He's going to be okay, Dawn."

She breathed in deeply. "I know."

Emotionally spent, the girls huddled on the uncomfortable hospital chairs next to Dawn. They twitched with weariness at the noise of Michael's moans, but soon fell asleep. Dawn couldn't help but see them as the three infants they once were, their eyes closed and little bodies wrapped in soft fleece hospital blankets.

On the other side of the bed, Deehan was gripping Michael's hands to steady and calm him. "You've got to come back to us," he whispered to Michael and moved his palm near Michael's injured head. "Don't get lost in there."

Dawn smiled faintly. This was probably the only time the two men had ever held hands.

Just then, Jade stirred from her nest of white blankets. She sat up and, rubbing her eyes, remembered where they were. "Mom," she whispered.

"Yeah, Hon?" Dawn whispered back, her voice stable.

"I think I'm going to walk around for a bit. I can't sleep. This room is freaking me out."

"Okay. Just don't pass out in the hallway," Dawn replied.

Jade gave her a fleeting look as if to say, *Really, Mom?*

I n the harsh fluorescent glare, Jade noted that the look of anxiety had dissipated from her mother's face. The semblance of serenity gave Jade permission to let go of the tension that had gathered in her shoulders and settled in her stomach. She pulled the arms of her sweatshirt down over her hands and walked out of Michael's room, closing the door behind her.

Being the oldest gave Jade a certain sense of responsibility and it showed in the way she carried herself. As she made her way to the bathroom and washed water over her skin, she could feel the weight of her place among her sisters. She looked in the mirror and inwardly complained about the dark circles under her eyes. She was afraid that she looked as tired as she felt, and it was difficult to have it confirmed by her reflection.

She roamed slowly down the hallway and stared out one of the broad windows overlooking a row of flimsy trees and a section of the grim parking lot. Unlike the boring setting below, so much had changed in merely a few hours. How could she possibly know what to think at this point? Her relationship with Michael—in fact, all of their relationships with Michael—had been tumultuous. Both she and Paige had moved out of the house to be with their real father because of it. Thinking back on the words she had said to her stepfather, some of the things she had done to intentionally hurt him, made her feel embarrassed and guilty.

"What are you doing?" Jade heard behind her. Without turning to see, she knew it was Paige.

"Staring. Obviously."

"At what, that Ford truck? Mesmerizing."

"What are you doing?" Jade asked, pressing her forehead against the glass and letting her breath gather in a fog.

"Mom said you took a walk. I didn't want to be in there anymore."

She turned to look at her sister, whose soft brown hair and light eyes reminded her of a gentler version of her father. "I think he'll be all right," she said. "At least Mom does anyway."

"Yeah," Paige agreed without enthusiasm. "I honestly don't know what to do if he doesn't pull through. Mom would lose it. Or I don't know, maybe she wouldn't."

"She's dead set on him making it," Jade continued, "and I think she might be right. For some reason it makes more sense for him to be okay than to die like that. He's too spiritual or something."

Michael's faith, or rather his way of expressing his faith, was a touchy topic. They found his approach irritating and pushy. It was, collectively, their least favorite characteristic of Michael's, particularly for Jade, who was the most wary of being shoved out of her mother's "new life" with God and Michael. She was already heading off to college and on the verge of adulthood when Michael slid into center stage with a whole production of new opinions and standards. Jade found his show-stealing performance frustrating and tiresome. Even so, she couldn't imagine that God would ignore the suffering of such an incredibly zealous follower.

When Michael first made an appearance in their mother's life, Jade had been happy for her. That was until the new couple, by Jade's estimation, got too serious too fast. Then her happy-for-mom attitude turned into a hostile-about-Michael resentment. Dawn had recently broken off an engagement with another man, and none of her daughters were ready for the new guy to play the serious boyfriend. Not that the girls were particularly fond of the previous fiancé either, but Michael was bigger than life and impossible to avoid.

Likewise, Paige wanted nothing to do with the relationship from the start. She moved in with her father in Green River before most of the major changes took place. But just like Jade, she was unable to escape the impact of life with Michael. Karsen, being young and still easy to please, hadn't been quite so mowed down by the experience, but the older girls had felt the brunt of their mother's fast-moving romance and every decision that went with it.

"Remember that first dinner?" Paige peered through the dingy glass and took a sidelong look at her sister. "My mouth was numb, and I could barely talk."

"Oh yeah—you had just gotten back from the dentist." In her mind, Jade pictured the fancy restaurant, the red table cloths, the posh décor, her mother's upscale dress, and then there was Paige, drooling foolishly across from her at the perfectly set table. "You needed a bib for the slobber."

"It only got worse from there." Paige's tone was humorous, but they both knew the truth was not as amusing.

It was an avalanche from the first dinner to the wedding, a landslide of unstoppable events that the girls were helpless to control. When the happy couple had announced the engagement, it was exactly that—an announcement. There was no question, no consideration; it was a declaration. "Michael and I are getting married," Dawn had told them with joy and complete confidence.

Matching her in total solidarity, Michael followed with, "And we are taking you girls to Hawaii for the wedding."

The girls were not impressed. It was as if they had been commanded to attend a funeral in Antarctica. For Paige and Jade, especially, it would be a journey made against their will. The picturesque tropical ambience couldn't compete with the doomsday cloud that hung over the discontented children. While Michael and Dawn exchanged vows on the isolated Hawaiian beach at sunset, the girls did their best to feign involvement—at least Karsen and Jade did. Paige looked away, rolling her eyes and breathing loudly to let her frustration be known.

After the ceremony, the photographer called for the girls to group around their mother. Jade had not missed the irony; they had tried to rally around their mom. They had tried to be a part of Dawn's new life, but even that was strange. Their "cool" mom had become a Christian. She was a different person with new rules and a new partner. Michael was in; they were out—simple as that.

For the final photos, the girls were directed to move further out of the way, and feeling the full significance of this request, Paige threw her bouquet down and stormed off.

"Why do you even want *him*?" she screamed.

This was the start of the huge family argument that poisoned the reception dinner and spilled awkwardly into every "first" family photo during the remainder of the trip.

The first family Christmas wasn't much better. Michael put Jade's gift under the tree a month before Christmas morning. She knew the medium-sized box wrapped in blue paper was a Bible, and for thirty days she dreaded having to open it and fake gratefulness for something he was always trying to push on her. Since they had been married, Michael felt he had a valid reason to force her into at least accepting a symbol of his religious beliefs. Every time she walked by the tree, Jade would glare at the blue rectangle with the bright red bow. When she opened it, sure enough, it was a Bible.

"Are you serious!?" She unleashed on Michael. It was inevitable. Jade had built up a lava pit of resentment over this gift, and by the time she untied the bow, she was ready to unravel. "I told you that I am *not* interested!"

Michael had shrugged it off. Now Jade hoped he would shrug this disaster off too. She put her weight against the window frame and faced the waiting room. A sigh floated from her lips.

As if reading her mind, Paige said, "If he doesn't make it, I'm going to feel horrible." She paused and explained, "I at least want to talk to him again. I hope I get the chance to say 'I'm sorry' for a few things."

With memories readily in mind, the girls returned from their walk. The monitor chirped erratically and the machine below hummed. Dawn was slouched in a chair, looking small and lonely as she watched the rise and fall of her husband's chest. The girls stared down at Michael's body. It was strange to see him so…helpless. This was the first time the girls had really seen him in a while, and suddenly, he wasn't Michael, *the man who stole our mother*. He was Michael, a man who, despite the pushiness and persistence, cared about them.

"I didn't know how much he mattered to me until you called," Jade said, addressing Paige but speaking to her mother as well. Dawn looked up and, without saying a word, walked over and held her girls in her arms. When she released them, she saw that Paige had been crying.

"He'll be fine," Jade said confidently. "God already saved his life."

It was early afternoon in the family waiting room. In walked a firm-footed man whose sharp green eyes studied a clipboard through thin metal frames. He carried himself with the confidence only years of hard-earned experience could instill. His lightly weathered face showed enigmatic signs of an amiable character, yet his air of professionalism removed any sentimentality.

As he began to speak, his rich German accent had a deeply reassuring resonance. "I am Dr. Meic Schmidt. Are you Mrs. Michael Pruett?"

Dawn extended her hand politely, "Yes."

He proceeded without hesitation, "It looks like the traction device has not helped to align Michael's spine and spinal cord. We will have to perform surgery to correct his spine fracture."

Nurse Paula had informed Dawn that Dr. Schmidt was renowned as one of the top neurosurgeons in the nation. He accepted Michael in transfer after they had diagnosed him. Dr. Schmidt agreed to perform the high-risk surgery. As Dawn reflected on the knowledgeable man standing before her now, something about his countenance assured her that he knew what he was doing.

Handing her a clipboard, he said, "I'll need you to sign off on the surgery. It could result in Michael being paralyzed."

By now, Dawn no longer questioned what she was signing. *Whatever it takes for Michael to be okay*, she confided to herself and scribbled her name resolutely.

Dr. Schmidt pushed his glasses farther up to the bridge of his nose and continued in a matter-of-fact tone, "Have you been briefed on the surgery?"

"Yes. I know that he has severe bruising and a broken neck, back, and ankle…" Dawn's voice trailed off. Just hearing the words come out of her mouth made her feel heavy-hearted and exhausted. She felt her body waver slightly beneath the burden.

Dr. Schmidt paused to study Dawn intently. "I can tell by your reaction and the expression on your face that either you haven't been briefed or don't know what's going on here."

Dawn paled, her chest becoming tight. *Don't take my peace…I just found it.* She looked around the room at Deehan and the girls. Each of them appeared depleted, yet strangely hopeful. She returned Dr. Schmidt's gaze, inhaling as she did so to build her confidence.

His look softened, as if he sympathized with her predicament. "Over eighty percent of people in his condition never walk again or become paraplegic. The spinal cord is so compromised the surgery could make him worse. Do you understand what I'm saying?"

"Yes, I understand," Dawn said in determination.

"Good," Dr. Schmidt said quickly. His stern countenance returned. "You must mentally prepare yourself for the worst-case scenario. We are doing this surgery to help Michael walk again, even if he loses some mobility in his neck."

Once he had finished explaining the tedious procedure and possibly tragic outcome, he intuitively paused before speaking, "Let me give you a clearer understanding: There is no doubt that the state in which he arrived at this hospital was miraculous given the high odds that he should have been completely paralyzed."

Miraculous... Dawn's thoughts echoed.

"But you must understand that his situation is still grave."

"Yes," she confessed.

"He'll be taken into surgery as soon as everything has been prepped." Dr. Schmidt turned to leave.

"Dr. Schmidt, wait," Dawn called to him.

He hesitated momentarily to shift his gaze toward her once again.

"Thank you."

He nodded in response and walked away. Dawn would not see Dr. Schmidt for ten hours.

It wasn't long before the nurses arrived to take Michael into surgery. As they began to move him, the weights attached to the cords stemming from the brace on his head swung precariously back and forth. His matted hair and unshaved face bobbed within the sheets. Ignoring the gruesome image, Dawn leaned down as the gurney passed.

"I love you," she whispered. Then she grasped Michael's hand until she was forced to let go.

Michael, oblivious to his predicament, gave a thumb's up as he was rolled away.

"Okaaay," Deehan spouted out. "He has no idea what's happening."

The two of them followed as part of Michael's entourage, supervising the group all the way to the ICU. They stopped next to a vending machine and huddled together in prayer. With both of their gazes fixed on the disappearing gurney, Dawn spoke softly. "This is it. This is where God has to come through for us."

Deehan nodded in silence while his posture deflated in defeat. Dawn knew it was difficult for him to watch his friend drift away into the control of others and the realm of the unknown. He slumped beside the vending machine and mentioned buying a Kit Kat, but none of the selections looked enticing. "I have no appetite for any of this," he said as he haltingly led the way back.

Once back in Michael's room, Dawn's body gave way to her lack of sleep. Nearly buckling, she rubbed her aching legs and lowered herself into an ugly gray chair. She ran her fingers through her tangled blonde hair and scrunched up a blanket into the shape of a pillow. Her eyes blinked slowly and eventually closed.

She awoke a few hours later to the sound of someone's footsteps. A young Asian woman had entered the room. Like Dr. Schmidt, she was dressed in white doctors' garb. Her hair was covered in a mint green hospital cap. She smiled graciously when she met their eyes, looking from one to the other. "I am Doctor Christina Sayama," she said. "Come with me, please."

Dawn leaned over to poke Deehan, whose eyes had also begun to open at the noise of the newcomer. They exited the room and followed the petite doctor through the ICU to an adjoining room filled with numerous unnamable machines, wires, and other technology. She drew their attention to several monitors that sat at eye level and pulled up an X-ray. Before them was a side view of Michael's spine and vertebrae. She pointed to his sixth notch in the line-up where the spinal cord was kinked like a hose, causing the cord to be misaligned.

Deehan fiddled with his phone to turn on the video camera and then pointed it at the screen as the young doctor began to describe Michael's X-rays.

"See how the spinal cord has stepped off the vertebrae?"

"Oh my God," Dawn muttered. "So you are going to reattach the spinal cord somehow?"

"No," she responded. "Let me show you where the spinal cord goes. Look at these films here." She downsized the first image and moved through more X-rays on the screen to show the inside of each of Michael's vertebra. "These are images of his head starting from the top down. Each one is a cut from the overall film. As we go down, we see his cervical, first vertebra, and so on."

In the X-rays, the spinal cord appeared like a distorted oval with vertebrae circling around it. The doctor maneuvered down through the digital imagery until suddenly the vertebra looked like it had been severed in half and the edges of the oval appeared like a haphazard cloud. She used her hand to indicate the variation. "So, that's where that step-off is. What happened is that there was a step-off on one side at one vertebra, but then there's *another* step-off on the other side of the next vertebra."

"How often do you see this type of damage?" Dawn asked, trying to decipher blurs of white and gray.

"We don't see it that often, but when we do, people usually have some type of long-term weakness. A lot of people are paralyzed or at least partially paralyzed."

"So, what are you saying?" Deehan was too tired to disguise his desire to simply cut to the chase.

Dr. Sayama smiled once again, "It's rare that we see people that are still neuro-intact—able to move and feel—with an injury like this. I think he must have a guardian angel."

Dawn gave the doctor a knowing look.

Deehan was already commanding attention as he waved his phone emphatically, "Wait, I don't think you said that loud enough. Could you repeat that on camera, please." Knowing that miracles were something the medical field rarely acknowledged, Dawn knew that Deehan felt compelled to capture this on video.

The doctor chuckled and repeated her statement again, "He has a guardian angel."

A shadowed, blood red apparition seemed to be weaving in and out around him, threatening and creeping in closer. It reminded Michael of something, a warning about death. The End Times.

He could sense the being near different parts of his body—his leg, the sides of his arms, the back of his head. If he could just fight it, maybe it would dissipate. He felt his arms swing upward in defense, but something held him down.

Other voices surrounded him too. Were they hostile? He tried to find them, but everything was black. Something held on tightly to his neck—were they hands? His mind was on fire. More images appeared, but never formed enough for him to understand.

The apparition slithered closer and whispered the familiar verse tauntingly, "A beast…"

Michael shuddered. He wanted to fight, but when he looked around again, he was surrounded by quiet, stone-faced children. They were all listening intently to an impassioned speaker. The speaker looked familiar. Michael knew him and the place. *Director Joe White. Kanakuk Kamp.* It was summertime, and Michael was ten years old.

The man's voice continued to speak the words of a fate-filled verse,

"It forced all people, great and small, rich and poor, free and slave, to receive a mark on their right hands or on their foreheads."

Why was he talking to them about the mark? Was he being forced to take it?

Fearfully, he opened his eyes to step away from the memory. The blinding light burned, and he raised his hands to shield his face. When he did so, the harrowing numbers flashed in front of him.

He yelled out.

It was on his forearm! The black numbers—666—had been scratched into his skin with ink and were dripping from the seeping wound.

The spiritual danger was visceral; Michael knew he must resist. He felt his body trying to escape, but he couldn't move. He heard himself speak out a promise to his parents, "I want to stand up for my faith, no matter what might happen to me. I'd rather have my arm cut off than to get that mark!"

"Michael, I believe you."

My father's voice! Michael sighed. He was in his father's station wagon again. The numbers were no longer on his forearm. He was safe.

"Yes," Michael affirmed. The conviction in his heart was strong, and he could see a barrage of promises written into the blackness before him.

"Do right and be rewarded."

"Work hard."

"Obey your parents."

"Go to college."

"Make money."

Michael told himself that he would do everything right.

Dawn was able to sleep more serenely than before Michael went into surgery. Deehan and the girls gathered then dispersed intermittedly while a dreamless Dawn rested. She awoke and slowly looked up to see Michael's sister, Michelle, standing beside her. Michelle's long blonde hair was casually pulled back into a ponytail, accentuating her thin frame. She peered down at Dawn reassuringly.

Dawn blinked to make sure that she was really there. "Finally!" She exhaled, yawned, and did her best to sit up straight in the chair. Michael's brother, Keeks, stood by Michelle. The duo had finally arrived. Relationship was a core value of the Pruett family, and Dawn had been swept into their charming household with love and grace. This foundation had trained Michael to recognize that lifelong relationships—both with family and friends—were perhaps the most important thing a man could have. His siblings had been his best friends throughout every season.

She stood up to embrace them. "I'm so glad you made it."

Keeks, being a doctor, made Dawn feel strangely confident in the otherwise daunting presence of the scurrying hospital staff. Now she would have someone with medical knowledge on her end of the conversation.

Keeks reached down and squeezed Dawn's shoulder. The vibrancy in his eyes resembled the bright look in Michael's, a look that she had admired often. It was as if the Pruett men had an internal gleam that said, "I'm a go-getter. I get things done." Dawn was comforted by the thought of Michael's self-motivated manner and the loved ones who had come to be his motivation. She noticed Matt Somers sitting next to Deehan. They were laughing and joking as usual. For a moment she was reminded of the pair goofing off at the park just the day before. It seemed like months ago. Somers caught Dawn's gaze, picked up his red baseball cap that had fallen to the floor mid-scuffle, and walked over to hug her.

"Matt, thank you so much for being here." To both Dawn and Michael, Somers was the quintessential Dad—reliable, gentle, possibly more patient than anyone Dawn had ever known. Having him there, even just seeing him in the room, gave her permission to believe that everything was going to be okay.

He winked at her in response, "Wouldn't miss it."

Dawn turned to find her daughters still fast asleep on the chairs.

"How long was I asleep?"

"It's late Monday night," Michelle answered as a small crease formed on her brow.

Deehan piped in, "He's been in surgery for about six hours so far. He should be out in a few."

Not fast enough, Dawn thought, wishing that she could speed up the clock.

As the family settled into the ever shrinking waiting area, Dawn and Deehan caught them up on what was happening. Dawn did her best to keep herself together, reporting the facts without emotion. She wanted to trust what she felt God had told her—Michael was going to be all right—yet the emotional trauma was taxing.

A few hours later Dr. Schmidt entered and stopped in the middle of the room, scanning for Dawn's face. His lips were curved upward in a soft smile.

Dawn breathed in to steady herself. Having learned the seriousness of Dr. Schmidt's nature, she interpreted that he had a positive report. Without thinking, she stood.

"Good news," he stated, the balls of his shoes lifting off the floor in a gesture of expectation.

"Yes?" Dawn answered.

"I don't often see people come out of this surgery so well. It went better than expected."

The room erupted in cheers. Deehan stood and stretched with liberation. Somers began to jostle and fake wrestle with him. Karsen buried her head in her mother's shoulder to cry in muffled relief. Jade and Paige exchanged looks of thankfulness while Michelle and Keeks called family members with the good news.

Dr. Schmidt raised his hand to reconvene them. "He has a long road to recovery ahead of him, but his spinal column and vertebrae are fully functional. So are his neck and back. With time, he is going to be *okay*." The emphasis he placed on that final word as he continued to gaze at Dawn sent a wave of gratitude through her mind.

"Thank you, God," Dawn uttered in astonishment of answered prayers. She had always known the truth, but as incongruous as it sounded, it was difficult for her to believe that God would actually come through. She had believed in her mind, but now she could also believe in her heart.

"The nerve pain will be intense," Dr. Schmidt warned. "It will be shooting throughout his body. This is the worst type of pain possible."

The room quieted down as Dr. Schmidt's countenance became more serious.

"You must also understand that trauma usually causes an altered mental state. We need to focus on getting the bleeding in his brain stabilized. It will be difficult to tell how his mental capacity is healing for a while yet."

Too caught up in a wash of relief, Dawn could hardly register Dr. Schmidt's comments. The exhilaration over Michael's successful surgery recovery was abruptly stunted by the one problem Dawn had feared from the start. If Michael survives was no longer the question. *Would Michael ever be Michael again?*

"Okay," she prayed under her breath. "Take him all the way through this. Don't let go until he's completely healed."

Michael was about to be brought back into the ICU. Deehan directed the traffic of friends and family through the labyrinth of corridors into the new recovery room. Then he and Dawn took their places on either side of Michael's bed. The others squished into various parts of the room, faces beaming with optimism. All were expectant, yet there was no amount of happy anticipation that could compete with the reality of Michael's appearance.

Dawn's eyes absorbed the image of her husband's battered body, and she shuddered involuntarily. He was completely disfigured, his neck swollen to three times its normal size. The massive amount of fluids that had been injected prior to the operation had caused bloating in every appendage, pushing each blue-black bruise brightly to the surface of his skin. Michael's hair was disheveled, greasy, and slicked back from surgery. His head lay on a blood-soaked pillow. Several IV cords were attached to each arm, and an oxygen line sprung from his half-open mouth. The tubes resembled a tangle of Christmas lights that trailed into different medical devices.

Dawn's thoughts escaped, and she said without thinking, "He looks like Frankenstein!"

Apparently, no one knew what to say in response. The room remained silent except for the shrill tweet of the monitor and the nurses' movements. They reattached clear tubes and liquid-filled bags while trying to minimize the physical evidence of trauma by adjusting the mattress and swapping out the filthy pillow for a fresh one. By the time the scrubs shuffled out, Michael was moving slightly and mumbling repeatedly, "Please hear me... please hear me."

Deehan eventually spoke out in bewilderment, "He looks trapped."

"He is trapped," Dawn whispered. "He keeps going in and out of consciousness. I can't imagine what that's like."

"Ignorance is bliss," Deehan contended while he slid a chair around to the end of the bed.

Scanning the length of his physique, Dawn confided, "Yeah, part of me hopes he doesn't know what's going on."

Michael stayed semi-conscious for a while; he seemed to be battling something in his dreams, but it had simmered to a mild squabble. Dawn couldn't let his words remove themselves from her mind. *"Please hear me."* What was going on inside his head?

Michelle moved to stand across the bed from Dawn. She was, like her brother, firm in her faith and unashamed of it. She took prayer seriously—Michelle would never let up—and, unlike some people who pray, she actually believed she was being heard.

With Michelle leading, both women lightly placed their hands on Michael's body, and for a few minutes, prayed for him to return to reality. His countenance started to slack and de-stress, yet his limbs still appeared to be scrambling incessantly in an effort to find a pain-free position.

She leaned down toward him and asked intuitively, "Who are you fighting? Are you fighting a lot of people?"

Michael answered her, "No, I'm fighting one person."

"Do you know him?" Michelle prodded him.

"Yes, I know him. And *you* know him."

She looked up and fixated on Dawn's eyes as if no one else was in the room. "I think this is as much a spiritual fight for him as it is a physical one. I'll be praying that whatever he's fighting, he wins."

Dawn wanted to believe that outcome for Michael, but too much supernatural talk scared her. She turned her attention to the grizzly stubble on her husband's cheeks and wished to see his charming smile.

"Deehan got it right," she mused. "He is trapped in there, fighting for his life. I just can't believe how crazy all of this is."

"It is strange to see him like this," Michelle said.

"I know. Surreal." She watched Michelle look tenderly at her brother. It had been a long time since he had been so vulnerable.

"I don't even remember the last time I saw him sleeping," Michelle commented. "This doesn't even register as the same person to me." She moved her hands to rest on Michael's chest and tapped her fingers to the rhythm of his heartbeat. Her expression changed, becoming softer, more thoughtful.

"What?" Dawn asked, hoping that they would find the answers they were looking for if they just kept talking.

"I was just thinking about when Michael was a boy. He was such a go-getter. Our parents never put unrealistic expectations on him, but Michael was determined in his own way." Michelle grinned. "All three of us were always so close. My kids just adore their Uncle Michael. That will never change."

She was quiet for a moment, and Dawn waited for her to keep talking. Hearing stories of Michael as a child was priceless and, especially now, comforting. Her mind filled with images from other stories Michael had told her about his adolescence. There was always something idyllic about his youth, at least compared with her own upbringing. When she pictured it, she couldn't help but hear the *Leave it to Beaver* theme song playing in her head. From her perspective, Michael didn't really become acquainted with disappointment until well into his twenties, the same disappointment many feel when love inexplicably dies a slow death.

Dawn knew the pain of divorce first hand; she also knew the pain of losing a loved one. Her husband, however, knew the pain of experiencing both at the same time. Based on the little information Michael had shared with her, Dawn understood how traumatic it had been for him when he was married to his first wife, Rachel, and his sister-in-law, Becky, died of cancer. She remembered him describing Becky as young, vibrant, and kind. Michael couldn't make sense of someone so full of life losing her life in such a cruel way.

His marriage had been failing at the time, and Michael couldn't make sense of it. He had married his high school sweetheart, after all, and as far as everyone else was concerned, they were the golden couple. Perhaps at one point in their lives they had been that couple, or at least had believed they could be. The two of them had shared every rite of passage growing up, even their sixteenth birthdays. By the time they tied the knot, both sides of their families had already merged into one. To say they were the shining stereotype of young love would not have been unjustified. Behind the scenes, however, their relationship was distressingly different. When Becky became ill, the truth surfaced.

"Michael, just leave," Rachel had told him out of suspended grief and fear, her sister fighting for her life on the other side of the wall. "Why do you want to be here? This isn't your family!"

But Michael couldn't leave. He had been completely invested in the future he imagined and was determined at the time to save it. He could be smart enough—or insistent enough—to make it work…somehow. If he didn't figure things out, no one would.

Dawn knew *that* was his greatest weakness: finally admitting defeat. Even after Michael was served divorce papers and the locks to his and Rachel's apartment were changed, he tried to hang on to the shreds. It took years for him to understand the dimensions of divorce, how truly damaging the experience had been for everyone involved. It was the move to Jackson Hole that finally forced him to let go. Yet moving away did not resolve the emotional devastation as he had hoped; Michael spent his first years in Jackson questioning everything he believed.

Though it hurt her to imagine her husband's heartbreak, she knew that Michael's past made their relationship all the more important to him. In one of those rare moments when he had opened up about Rachel, she told him that perhaps he had come to Jackson to take a good job offer, but instead God had opened that door for him to move on and gain perspective. How could he have known how hurt he was without enough distance to see his past for what it was?

Dawn considered those words again as she looked at her husband, unconscious, fighting. He always tried to see and plan so far ahead, yet it had only led him here…to more suffering. He never saw *this* coming. Or did he? Dawn wondered if perhaps he had a clue because of what he had written in that email. He knew something hard was coming down the road. He just didn't know it would be quite so literal.

Michelle's voice broke into Dawn's thoughts. "You okay?"

Dawn looked up in surprise. "What do you mean?"

"Your face changed. You seem a little…" Michelle stopped herself. "He's going to pull through this. I know it."

Dawn believed her, but she couldn't shake her questions. *What if…?* Or better yet, *Why?* "I don't understand any of it," she finally said to Michelle in resignation. "Why bad things happen to good people, why some people die, and others survive—why this happened to Michael at all. I guess I'm simply glad he is fighting for his life."

Michelle's look softened. "I don't understand it either, but God does. In time, He always reveals the answers to us. I remember telling Michael years ago to simply trust…something good *can* come out of the bad. It's easy to trust when everything is going well, but it's called *faith* for a reason. I don't have the words to comfort you. Ask God your hard questions and wait for His answers."

Dawn nodded, wanting to agree. Was it really *trust* if it disintegrated at every moment of uncertainty? The reality of Michael's critical condition in front of her seemed to war against the hope Michelle offered. Was trust truly as simple as that? As simple as trusting that God had answers to her questions? Or did trust require something else—for her to simply let go of the *why?*

Michael believed he was in a trance, a dream world with no beginning or end. There were only scenes, moments of his life strewn before him. He couldn't choose which he saw, and which he didn't, but at least the darkness was diminishing.

He watched himself loping along a backwoods trail with his dog, Willie. They maneuvered over boulders, through gullies, beside creeks, and then finally left the trail to forge out into the wild.

Suddenly the backdrop changed. Michael was still in the woods, only now he was on a mountaintop overlooking green-forested hills. He could see someone—a duplicate version of his own form looming in the distance. The strange scene reminded him of something, but he couldn't place it. The man's arm was raised high above his head, his hand grasping a crude flint knife.

Then Michael understood. How could he not? He had heard the story many times since Sunday School. Abraham atop Mount Sinai—Isaac on the altar. Michael watched from afar.

Like any nightmare, the face of the victim continuously changed, transforming into the faces of people he knew until the morphing stopped, and Michael saw himself helplessly lying on the table. He screamed out.

Nothing changed. No one could hear him. The large hooded figure was about to jab the knife into his chest. Michael squinted against the sunlight above and saw his own face hiding within the shroud.

He heard the words, "I give, and I take."

"Please!" he screamed. "Let me go!" All Michael could see was the dagger and the blue sky beyond, "I'm begging you!"

He felt agonizing pain streak throughout his body. In the next instant, he was suspended in light, and he knew in his gut that this was the end.

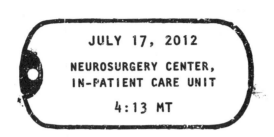

JULY 17, 2012

NEUROSURGERY CENTER,
IN-PATIENT CARE UNIT

4:13 MT

When Michael regained consciousness, he was exceptionally agitated. His eyes were wild and red, and he writhed like a feral animal in a cage. He cried out in a voice that was supposed to be commanding, but was actually raspy and fairly weak, "Get me out of here!" He looked furiously at those surrounding his bed as though each of them were responsible for his imprisonment.

The same scenario played out over and over again. Michael would call out, "I have...been...captured! I am being tortured. Do you hear me? Let me go!" Bloodshot eyes would blink in disbelief, then Michael would mumble explanations about why he needed to be rescued. When the onlookers didn't respond, he would lash out with expletives.

Dawn stood by his side unflinching, feeling stronger than twenty-four hours before. "Michael, you have to stay here."

"No!" He recognized his wife, but he was unsure about the rest of the visitors. He would squint, trying to identify a face only to give up in frustration and curses.

On and off, the monitoring nurses, donned in floral scrubs, would saunter in and check his vitals.

Michael grumbled with their every movement, and Dawn could tell that his irritation was escalating.

Once in a while between her other duties, Paula would check in with them. Despite long shifts, she never lost her charm. Her rosy cheeks matched her garments and maternal manner. "Mrs. Pruett," she'd say. "This is normal. Everything's fine. It's a natural reaction."

"Who is *she*?!" Michael yelled once, referring to Paula. Dawn didn't know what to say, but Paula merely peered over her shoulder. Not satisfied with their reaction, Michael lifted his plaster cast leg and swung it out over the edge of the bed toward Paula. It was a laborious attempt to fight back.

"Yeow!" Paula yelled loudly as she dodged the flailing attack. Her yelp only served to galvanize Michael's belligerent efforts to break free.

Dawn covered her mouth in horror. Thankfully, both Deehan and Somers stepped into the room. Seeing their friend in a violent rage, they tried to pin him down.

Dawn grabbed Paula's shoulder and said desperately, "I am so sorry!"

Paula ran her fingers along the edge of her wrinkled sleeve and shrugged, "Like I said, this is normal, and I'm used to it."

Dawn looked over pleadingly at Deehan and Somers and, in a voice that was louder than she had intended, asked, "How in the world am I ever going to be able to take him home? He's dangerous!"

Somers returned Dawn's look with an assured observation. "He's made it so far. Now it's time for us to pray for his personality to come back."

"And quickly, I might add," Deehan chimed in.

Displaying a compassionate nature, Paula delved into the conversation, "Mrs. Pruett, he really is going to be okay. Physical trauma to the brain causes emotional trauma. We'll restrain him, and that should help a bit." She motioned for Deehan and Somers to keep holding him while she strapped down his arms and legs to the metal frame.

The two men looked dubious as Paula kindly advised, "You might want to keep distracting him."

Dawn nodded, but inside wondered if Michael's character would be impacted permanently. She sighed and geared up to address her husband, "Michael, you need to listen to me because—" She cleared her throat and raised her voice to be more convincing. "Because I am...really...smart. I'm telling you, it's best for you to stay here." She chuckled in spite of herself and then confirmed how ridiculous she sounded when she saw the smirk on both Deehan and Somer's faces.

"That's some solid logical reasoning," Deehan teased.

"Actually," Michael answered in a matter-of-fact tone, "you're *not* smart, and you are betraying me! You're all in this together!"

Deehan and Somers burst out in laughter. Somers' blue eyes sparkled beneath his baseball cap, "That's more like it, Michael!"

Dawn shook her head and tried to laugh with them, but she doubted how much she could tolerate. *What kind of transformation were they in for and for how long?* She settled to the floor, closed her eyes against the painful possibilities, and put her head between her hands. She could hear Michelle talking with her girls and Deehan and Somers jesting with

Michael. She finally lifted her head and watched as Michael's two best friends took charge. Deehan secured a forearm to prevent the IV from being disengaged, and Somers laced his fingers through Michael's to be comforting.

Confused, Michael thought that they were there to free him from his captive state. He tried to swing around, sit up, and jump off the bed. "Get me outta here, man!" he yelled.

"Sorry, bud. This is for your safety." Somers had a calming tone that was equally determined.

Michael became manic, thrashing his arms and legs as if electrocuted. "God dammit!"

Deehan cut in as he pinned him, "Hey, just because you were hit by a truck doesn't mean you get to be an asshole. We are here to *help* you!"

Michael reached up still thinking he was about to be set free, his hands clasping Deehan and Somers.

Again, the two men wrestled him down into the pile of sheets. Suddenly, Deehan's voice grew louder in warning, "I see that look in his eye!"

Dawn knew instantly what he meant—it was the look a man gave before he threw a punch.

"Screw you, dammit!" Michael screamed, and the punching ensued.

"Why are you mad at me?" Deehan goaded him. "I'm here to help you."

Dawn sighed and looked up at Michael's friends. "Even if he keeps physically recovering, I can't take this wild animal home and care for him. What am I going to do?"

Deehan turned away from the bed to face her. "I wouldn't worry about it right now. I recognized something different in his eyes this time anyway. He's in there...somewhere. He's not quite as lost as we may have thought."

Deehan and Somers's intervention was a great assistance to the staff and family. Having Michael's two best friends use their strength to steady him eventually helped to steady everyone. Michael clung to them, beginning to understand through the torment that the people holding him down were not his enemies.

When Dawn witnessed this, tears stung her eyes. What men would stay by their friend's side day and night—seeing him at his absolute worst—and still choose to hold his hands just to keep him composed?

The milieu of aggression continued. Michael would think he was being freed and then become furious when he recognized that his friends were indeed his security guards. The cursing and the rage returned, and it took several days before Deehan pinpointed a pattern in Michael's behavior. His erratic personality increased significantly whenever he was physically uncomfortable. If he had to relieve himself or was simply squished in the mattress, he would react with anger. After figuring this out, whoever was in the room would help him adjust, and then Michael would settle back down.

The nights turned into days and the days into nights again. Despite the weak coffee, cafeteria meals, and uncomfortable chairs, the hospital started to feel like a makeshift home. Dawn had been offered rest at a local house, but she wouldn't let herself be pulled away from her husband. Keeks and Michelle had to get back to their families, and Somers was set to leave soon as well. For the time being, Michael's immediate family and his two best friends remained together, fighting for his full recovery through prayer. Michael was moved several times; his level of intensive care was constantly changing. Most of the time, Dawn and Michelle would pray for Michael, and when they got tired, Deehan and Somers took over.

"I've focused my prayers on his mental recovery because I like how this guy thinks," Somers mentioned to Dawn. "Every doctor who has talked to us about his X-rays said that if they saw his injuries and had no other information to go on, they would assume that he was dead or paralyzed."

"I know that most people would not have survived," Dawn agreed, and then added quietly, "But I want his personality to survive too."

"Well, I gotta tell you this is the closest thing to a real miracle that I've ever experienced," Somers encouraged. "Now, if Michael can just start being Michael again."

Michael's constant swearing felt unnatural. Each curse word was an audible shockwave that scared Dawn and the girls. These episodes were happening so frequently, however, that Dawn felt her defenses wear down. She couldn't help but consider all of the other issues in her and Michael's life. Michael was nearing financial disaster when they were engaged and married, which plagued them during their first years of marriage. Now that he was out of commission and she was on sabbatical, what was going to happen? How could they afford to pay all of his medical bills?

The practical questions piled up, but before she went into a full-blown anxiety attack, Dawn finally escaped outside. She decided to get some fresh air and let the sunlight warm her face.

On her way to the lobby, she noticed other families. Most of them were there for loved ones who had not received miracles like Michael had. They looked damaged, depressed, and even afraid. They were suffering in the unknown and possibly going to lose someone they loved. Michael was on his way to recovery. Dawn empathized with every one of them. Each time she passed another waiting family, she reminded herself of her previous resolution, to let go of the *why*.

Cajoling herself out of her questions, she whispered aloud as she walked out into the sun, "Please, God." The light was overwhelming. She didn't want to consider the negative possibilities. She simply didn't have the strength. One word seemed to filter through her thoughts and make its claim above the others—*trust*.

Dawn breathed in deeply. "I don't need to know how this is going to work out. I just need to focus on all the good that is happening, not the good that hasn't happened...yet."

" Why?" Michael heard himself ask. "Why are you doing this to me?"

Silence.

Then he remembered the terrorizing vision of Abraham. His back recoiled, but he was still strapped to the hard stone on that fatal mountain. If he somehow freed himself and jumped, would he—?

Something else demanded his attention, as if forcing him to remain still. It spoke to him, "You still haven't learned."

"What? I don't understand?" He called into the empty air.

Again, silence.

Michael struggled against the strappings, but realized that his efforts were useless. "I get it. I can't control this." On one side of the boulder the landscape looked like Paradise, yet the fall would be brutal. On the other side, sheer granite stared back at him. "I give up."

He let his body grow limp in compliance. He felt so tired. As he did so, a sense of peace replaced exhaustion. Suddenly, he felt a burst of vitality, and inexplicably he wept. He cried for every failure and every trial he had ever survived over the previous twenty years. Each difficulty was drenched in the memory of self-reliance and loneliness. For better or worse, he was stuck in that state of surrender—perhaps eternally—and he couldn't even move his hand to wipe his face.

Deehan had taken the initiative to let the community of Jackson Hole know about Michael's accident. The newspaper kept everyone informed, and the comments and concern flooded in. The fact that so many cared about Michael's recovery meant more to Dawn than she could express. She believed that one day Michael would walk along the streets of Jackson and someone would stop him.

"Hey, aren't you the guy that almost died in the motorcycle accident?" They'd ask. "How were you saved?"

She smiled to herself and sighed.

Deehan looked up from his computer.

"This could be so different," Dawn stated, sipping her coffee and placing the other cup she had retrieved on the table next to Deehan.

"Thanks. What do you mean?"

"I could be attending his funeral, and instead I am helping him with his physical therapy."

Michael woke up, shifted his body, and groaned.

Deehan jeered and called to him, "Hey, Schmichael."

To their astonishment, Michael replied, "Hey, Schmatty!"

"Maybe he's starting to remember," Dawn suggested, laughing. "Keep talking to him."

Deehan set down his laptop and stood up next to Michael's bedside. "Do you remember what happened?"

Michael sounded coherent and normal. "Not exactly."

"Do you want me to tell you what happened to you?" Deehan asked, and then added an aside, "For the hundredth time."

"Yes."

"You've been in a car accident. You're in the hospital to recover."

But the instant was gone. Michael began to resist lying down, tearing away from Deehan's grip. "Why won't you help me out, man?"

Just then a new nurse came in and set a tray of food on the table by Michael's bed. "All right, time for you to eat." She picked up a small container of Jell-O, dug the spoon into it, lifted the spoon to his mouth, and coaxed him.

Michael violently turned his head away, causing the nurse to lose her grip on the spoon, which went flying to the floor, spilling Jell-O everywhere.

"I'm sorry," Dawn apologized to the nurse. This wasn't the first time Michael had refused to eat.

The nurse shrugged. "If he won't eat, Mrs. Pruett, we might need to put him on a feeding tube."

Deehan interjected, "We'll keep trying."

The nurse said hesitantly, "I have to warn you. Based on the way Michael is right now with his movements and resistance, they will most likely have to induce a coma in order to keep the tubes in."

Dawn's face went blank. "Another coma?"

"Is that really necessary?" Deehan interrupted.

"He'll just pull out the tubes at this point," the nurse explained.

"But what would that do to him, the coma, I mean?" Dawn asked, still trying to be calm.

"Well, I won't lie to you," the nurse said, addressing her captive audience. "It's always a risk for any patient. Especially for someone with a head injury like Michael's."

Dawn and Deehan shared a look.

"We'll get him to eat," Deehan said in a determined, gentle tone.

Suddenly, their attention turned to a knock on the open door and a deep voice called out to them from behind, "Well, hello there."

Dawn looked over her shoulder to see Mike, her pastor from River Crossing Church, standing in the doorway. The minute her eyes met his, she felt vulnerable, like Mike could see all of her fear and doubt. She breathed in nervously and stood to embrace him. "Pastor Mike!"

Mike hugged Dawn, Deehan, and the girls, and then proceeded to walk to Michael's side.

The nurse retrieved the spoon from the floor, and Pastor Mike watched her as she cleaned up the mess on the floor. "I see what's happening here," he teased Michael in a quiet manner.

Dawn reached over to touch Michael. "The trauma to his brain has caused him to be violently emotional at times, and he hasn't been eating well."

The nurse cut in, "He hasn't been eating at all."

"They're not going to let him go home until he starts eating on his own," Dawn said, her own thoughts continuing, *Not that I would know how to take care of him like this anyway.*

"Hi there," Pastor Mike greeted Michael.

Dawn could tell that Michael recognized Pastor Mike but he wasn't fully cognizant.

Michael looked up. "Hi," he echoed, and then added, somewhat angrily, "What are *you* doing here?"

"I came to see you. You're here because you've been in an accident, but God spared your life, and you are going to get better." Then he placed his hand on Michael's arm.

"Don't touch me!" Michael demanded. "Get your hands off, God dammit!"

Dawn jolted into a standing position and her face turned red. "I am *so* sorry, Pastor. He's been—"

But Pastor Mike remained stationary. "Really, I am not offended," he said, smiling and waving his free hand toward Dawn, a gesture to keep her from apologizing.

After the nurse cleaned the spoon, Dawn scooped up the remaining Jell-O from Michael's tray. "Michael, it's your wife. I'm asking you to eat this one bite for me," she pleaded.

Michael looked at her blankly as she moved the spoon toward his closed mouth. "No."

"Yes," she emphasized.

"Maybe try doing the airplane thing," Deehan offered, but Dawn only looked at him smugly.

"Please eat, Michael. It's one bite. For me." Dawn was worn out, and the emotional and physical exhaustion was starting to take its toll. Tears welled up as she held the spoonful in front of her husband's face, and her hand started shaking.

"Let me try," Pastor Mike suggested calmly.

Embarrassed, Dawn handed him the spoon.

Pastor Mike brought a spoonful of wiggling red gelatin to the front of Michael's face.

The nurse watched casually from the end of the bed.

"Michael, listen to me," Pastor Mike began. "You need to eat or they are going to put you on a feeding tube."

Michael began to be combative again. "No!"

In a commanding yet gentle manner, Mike continued. "This is Pastor Mike talking to you. You need to eat this. I want you to eat this. Your wife wants you to eat this. Heck, *Jesus* wants you to eat this." He lifted the spoon to Michael's mouth.

After looking back-and-forth between Mike and the spoon, Michael finally opened his mouth and ate. When Pastor Mike lifted the spoon again, Michael tried to move his head away.

"I'm speaking to *you*, Michael, to the real you. We all want you to eat this so you can get better and go home."

Surprisingly, Michael attempted to nod but couldn't, so he simply said, "Okay."

"*Okay?*" Dawn repeated and laughed.

The nurse watched with relief as Michael continued to eat. "That's good enough for me, Mrs. Pruett," she said, smiling compassionately at Dawn.

When Michael was done eating, Pastor Mike stepped closer to Dawn, put his arms around her, and drew her in. At this, the others slowly made their way out of the room, leaving them alone with the nurse, who eventually excused herself without much notice.

"I know you are overwhelmed," Pastor Mike began. "And you've had to make some really difficult decisions in the last few days," he added.

"I'm so grateful he's alive, but..." Dawn cleared her throat. "I don't know what to do if he doesn't get better. What if he won't eat, and they put him in a coma that makes it worse? What if he never comes out of it?"

Silent tears began to fall as Dawn let herself break down completely. Pastor Mike was a presence of peace for her, and she felt safe enough—and drained enough—to let someone else be strong for her. She exhaled deeply, wiped away the tears, and began to tell him everything—every thought and emotion from the moment she first knew Michael was in trouble, and every discussion, decision, and conversation with the medical staff. She told him about the trauma of not knowing his full diagnosis or whether or not he would survive at Saint John's; how fear and hope pulled her in every direction each minute; the unbelievable joy at knowing that Michael would walk again and her uncertainty about Michael's full mental recovery.

She simply let Pastor Mike hold her until she no longer heaved with tears, her breaths were deep and calm, and her eyes were dry. She sighed and looked up at him. "Thank you. I'm sorry about your shirt," she said, grabbing a tissue. "It's all wet."

"Not a problem at all." Pastor Mike looked away as Dawn collected herself. "You know," he began, "I have watched Michael come through a lot of seasons in his life. He's always been bigger than life, or at least someone who loves life. But I've also seen him strive for everything he has."

Dawn watched her husband as Mike spoke to her. He was right. *Strive* was a good word for it.

"He's a great guy. He's generous and fun loving and hard working, but," he said, moving closer to Michael's bed and grabbing the side of it with his hand, "he's incredibly independent. I know that Michael would take that as a compliment, but I don't mean it as one."

Dawn wanted to speak, but she was too tired.

"He has tried to make his own way and to be the best at it. He's seen some highs and lows; we all do. He has always believed in God, even trying to be the best Christian as though there could be such a thing. He's always wanted to serve God, but he's never really yielded to Him. This might be part of the struggle."

Dawn nodded and thought back to the conclusions she had come to a few days before. "I agree." She was starting to understand. Suffering happened. Tragedy happened. Pain wouldn't ever be eliminated from human existence until Heaven. So what were people supposed to do with it?

Mike said reassuringly, "I don't believe God ever creates this kind of suffering. I don't subscribe to the idea that God makes us sick or takes away our loved ones to teach us lessons. Just being born is hard work, and it doesn't get easier. I know that He uses every circumstance, even the bad ones, to show us how good He is. I have no doubt that Michael will pull through this, but it's going to be a fight."

Dawn sat down in her designated chair and reached over to hold Michael's hand.

"In some ways he reminds me of Jacob," Mike continued, "struggling for every good thing in life—with his brother, his father, his boss—but it's not until he wrestles with God in the desert that he actually changes."

Dawn imagined Jacob's battle with God. Perhaps people weren't meant to avoid problems. Perhaps those problems were meant to bring people closer to God. Perhaps God was "righting" Michael's path. Michael had tried so hard to surrender to God time and again, yet he could never quite do so. He would always tell God, "I've got this. Really. I can fix it."

Michael, simultaneously agitated and curious, kept darting his eyes from Pastor Mike to his wife without saying a word.

"He must recognize you," Dawn noted. "He seems a lot calmer with you here."

Mike nodded, "I knew I was supposed to come." Part of Mike's job as a pastor was to travel often to speak at various churches worldwide. He was busy and rarely available for hospital visits, especially a visit five hours away from Jackson. "It's difficult to explain, but I felt compelled to come here. I knew there was the possibility that he could be paralyzed or even die. Only severe cases are brought to Salt Lake."

"Well, I'm glad you came." Dawn paused and then added hesitantly, "Would you do me a favor and check in with my girls? I think they might be a little more open than they've been before."

"I'd love to," Mike said, opening the door for the two of them to leave the room.

Dawn waved for Deehan—who was standing in the hallway talking to an attractive nurse—to come back into Michael's room.

Deehan acknowledged her and wrapped up his conversation. "I'm going to step out for a minute," Dawn explained.

"I'll take over," he answered, grabbing her shoulder and giving it a squeeze.

Pastor Mike kept his arm around Dawn as they walked into the waiting area. The girls knew him from being forced to go to church, yet their discomfort with a religious leader didn't seem to matter now.

Dawn took a seat nearby, far enough to let her daughters talk freely without wondering if she could hear. It was getting late, and most of the other families had either gone to a hotel for the night or were already sleeping in the waiting area. From the expressions on her daughters' faces, Dawn could guess what they were talking about with Pastor Mike: remorse for their harsh words and rebellious actions toward Michael, pain from not having expressed that they actually cared, and uncertainty about how they could possibly return to life if Michael didn't recover.

Paige fidgeted in her seat and finally got up and walked toward her mother. She had an innocent, almost bashful look on her face, which Dawn would never have described as typical.

Dawn waited breathlessly to see what her middle child—the one who had given Michael the most trouble—wanted to say.

Paige uttered softly, "I want to go talk to Michael," she said.

"Okay, honey," Dawn said, standing up, stretching slightly, and taking her daughter's hand. Pastor Mike, Jade, and Karsen followed behind them.

As Paige stood quietly beside Michael, who was tired and therefore less aggressive, she uttered, "I...I love you," with a tone of mild embarrassment. It was the first time she had ever said the words to him.

"You do?" Michael looked casually at her. "Sweet!"

Paige frowned. "Mom...I...." Then she began to cry.

"It's okay, baby." Dawn tried to comfort her. Michael had an amused look on his face.

"Kind of ironic, isn't it?" Dawn said, starting to laugh.

Paige nodded and let her mother wrap her arms around her.

"He just can't comprehend what you are saying right now."

Jade and Karsen joined them at Michael's side, and each began to speak to him freely, even though—or perhaps because—he couldn't understand the significance of their words.

Paige finally addressed her mother. "I just...I just never wanted to betray Dad. I felt like if I accepted Michael, Dad would think I didn't love him anymore. All I really wanted was for the two of you to get back together. Michael got in the way of that."

"I know."

All three siblings clung together around their mother. Dawn could tell that Paige was trying to stifle her tears. She didn't enjoy being vulnerable.

"I just need...Michael to know...that I care," Paige continued.

"He does, Paige. I promise," Dawn assured her. "And you can tell him yourself when he wakes up for real."

Michael lay with the back of his head pressed against an upright pillow, his eyes closed. The pain throughout his body, minimized by medication, was still strong enough to distract him from his surroundings. But he also felt the brightness from the light outside. The heat of the sun on his skin blended with the sound of conversation around him. It was comforting, as if something deep and dark had occurred but had not lasted. He felt like he was under water, the sound of his wife's voice distant, her words unclear.

Dawn... A flash of metal scraping the ground, the sound a deafening roar. He had screamed. He felt frightened, scared that she had died.

The movement of his thoughts were oddly both subtle and abrupt— an unnerving mix of a familiar stream of consciousness that took sharp turns into questions and memories he could only describe as not really belonging there, making his mind feel foreign and somewhat dull. Every image was dissolving and moving past him like debris in a river, yet he was still somehow with each, watching it float by.

Michael knew he was lying next to his wife, but he also knew she was not lying next to him. Where was he? Why was he lying down alone? What had happened? He did not know. How could he possibly find the answers to questions that never fully formed?

"Michael!"

He opened his eyes. "Yes?" It was Dawn.

"Can you hear me?"

"I can hear you," he answered, closing his eyes again.

"How are you feeling?" she asked, but Michael didn't know where to start. His entire body ached. His mind was slow. His thoughts were morphing into other thoughts before he could fully grasp them.

"Shape-shifting," he mumbled to himself. The only time he remembered feeling anything close to this was when he was young. Oftentimes as a child he'd wake up from lucid or nightmarish dreams to adult conversations in another room. His mind would create images to make sense of their stories.

He heard Dawn talking to others, and everyone was agreeing about miracles. The words met him, but meant nothing. He blinked and looked at the forms of people around him blankly. He opened his mouth to speak but realized he had nothing to say.

Dawn quit talking.

He knew she was waiting for him to say something. He looked down at his hands and then his legs covered in white sheets.

"What...happened?" he asked.

Dawn sighed. "Well," she started. Her voice sounded methodic, like she had been reciting the explanation over and over again. "You were in an accident. You have been in surgery and recovering for the last week. We're going home very soon."

He stared at her with the same look of confusion he instinctively knew he had given her before. He had been told more than once, but the only thing he remembered was a motorcycle ride and the way it felt to have her holding onto him as they made their way back home from Yellowstone.

Michael closed his eyes. Images of riding his motorcycle filled his mind. He could see the trees clearly; the wind was against him. He was gaining speed.

The drive was quiet, he remembered. The image of speeding close to water came to him, and as he made a sharp turn, he saw something—maybe a bird—flying right at him.

He woke suddenly, startled, before it struck. Had he been sleeping again? He could smell something foul, like an overstuffed basket of dirty clothes or old cafeteria food. He felt soiled, unclean. Attempting to lift himself up from the bed, he realized he couldn't.

"Michael, wait!" He heard Dawn say. He cried out and then let his muscles relax again.

"I...I need to take a shower," he murmured, feeling exasperated.

"Okay, we'll help you," she said. And then Deehan was by his side too, pulling him up from the bed. Why was Deehan here? He wanted to thank him, but he didn't have the strength. His wife on one side and his best friend on the other, all three struggled to the adjoining bathroom.

Michael felt his feet move forward slightly and then drag. Move forward little by little, and then collapse. Reaching the bathroom seemed to take forever, and he did not feel rewarded when they arrived. It was small and sterile like an empty cubicle of white tile that had never been used.

Dawn turned on the light.

Michael was shocked at his reflection. There he was, tall, broad-shouldered, and strong, but his dark honey hair had chunks missing, and he was cut up and marked unrecognizably. Something terrible had happened or had been happening. Perhaps it wasn't over.

Deehan left them alone, and Dawn began to slowly disrobe him from the blue hospital gown. He was surprised that he was naked underneath.

"Are you okay?" she asked gently.

He hesitated as his thoughts started to stitch together.

Dawn was quiet. "Michael," she began again in more of a question than a statement.

"Yeah?"

"What are you thinking right now?"

"I'm not thinking. It's like I can see things in a fog. My thoughts come to me right as I pass them, and then they aren't there anymore. I don't think...I'm well," he said, tears forcing their way out as he tried to hold his head in his hands, but couldn't.

"Yes, Michael. You're recovering. Trust me. You've been looking at me differently today," she said. "You looked like you were...*here*."

He leaned on her heavily then, and she helped him step up into the tiny plastic shower. He felt the water pour over him. His body tingled and stung. His skin felt thin, agitated. He half expected the water to seep past his flesh into his blood. He wanted to wash off everything, whatever had happened. He began sucking in air and holding his breath to deal with the pain.

"Michael?" Dawn questioned. He could sense worry in her tone, but it hurt too much to move his head toward her. He slowly lifted his hands to place his palms against the tiles and lean his head against the wall. Clear liquid cascaded down his back. He glanced downward and saw that brown mixed with crimson, staining the water.

"What happened to me?" he asked, but he already knew. It was a chorus he had heard many times. *You were in a motorcycle accident. You were hit by a truck. It's a miracle you are alive. It's a miracle you can walk.*

His feet slipped and his left side smacked into the shower door with a resounding crash.

"Michael!"

His eyes shifted.

Dawn dashed into the shower fully dressed. She swiftly slid her arms around his torso and held him carefully.

The dark marks on his body dissolved, splashing onto her. She obviously didn't care. His blue eyes held hers. She knew that he knew, that he understood now. She cried for him, with him. He had never seen her like this before. She was always so strong. She was always enough, enough for him.

"You're okay. Thank God, you're okay. Dawn, I was so afraid..."

"I wasn't with you, Michael. You dropped me off before you collided with the truck downtown."

"I...I don't remember anything," he choked out as he sobbed.

Words tumbled out of Dawn's mouth creating splashes of colored scenes in his mind. "You survived, Michael. You should have died. You should have been paralyzed. But you weren't." She continued explaining what had happened, but Michael couldn't focus.

The only thing he could hear in his head were the words, "You need to let me win," but were those his words or someone else's? Who had Michael been struggling with, or better yet, who had been struggling with him?

```
┌─────────────────────────────┐
│      JULY 26, 2012          │
│       HIGHWAY 15            │
│        9:54 MT              │
└─────────────────────────────┘
```

Michael imagined the scenery they were passing on the drive home—the tall, brown rocky crags that lined the highway, the small clusters of pines that were dark green, mysterious, and standing alone against the backdrop of barrenness. He had a sudden inexplicable urge to see his parents, or was it the sudden conviction that if he were to open his eyes now, they would be there in the car, driving him to camp like they did every summer so many decades ago? Michael did not open his eyes to check. He knew they would not be there beside him; Dawn would be.

Before he was discharged, the doctors gave him marching orders. He was not allowed to drive or go back to work for a month, and he needed as much rest as possible.

"After head injuries, stress heightens the chance that the brain will not heal quickly," he and Dawn were told. The nurses quizzed Michael about what year it was, where he was, who the president was. Michael could understand and answer them, but if Dawn asked him to repeat instructions, he would sometimes forget things and make up answers. That was not reassuring.

He couldn't keep track of time, and they soon reached the cul-de-sac at the end of their road in Jackson. He opened his shuttered eyes to watch Dawn slowly make the sharp right turn up the steep incline to their home. To the left of their driveway, nearly ninety-degree steps led up to their covered porch. Their two-story log cabin rested on a several hundred-foot bluff above downtown Jackson Hole.

Once they arrived home, Michael felt more relaxed. The cabin had been his residence long before Dawn and the girls entered his life, and it brought a sense of comfort with it. The only thing still completely unfamiliar was his own reflection in the mirror. He never expected to see scars or deep blood bruises looking back at him. What was worse, sometimes he had to remind himself of why they were there. He would ask Dawn and watch as her face lost its brightness and listen to her words that were full of weariness. He wondered if he should feel ashamed of himself or guilty. He did not know.

Dawn helped him set up everything he needed in their bedroom, from his medicine and ice packs to books, a television, and snacks. Michael was grateful to be out of the hospital and in his own bed.

The last time he had been in a hospital was for Becky, his sister-in-law, after her stroke. And before that was...*Rachel*. Michael felt the name run through his body. He remembered being in the hallway with his ex-wife standing in front of him, letting him know he was no longer welcome there. Her mother was there too, and after watching one daughter die, she told Michael she wouldn't stand by and let her other daughter stay in an unhappy marriage. At the time, when his first marriage was slipping away from him, he had believed only a couple of changes were needed to save it. He made promises and determined to stick to them.

"I couldn't fix it," he said unaware to the empty room, shutting his eyes.

Rachel. The dissolution of his first marriage brought Michael to Jackson Hole. His friends told him he was escaping. Maybe he was, but he believed in fresh starts. During those first few weeks in Jackson, he looked out at the mountains, drove past elk, hunted with friends, and went for runs that helped him realize that he was finally alone and that he could create a new life. He had decided to start over in Jackson Hole, and he never looked back.

Jackson also offered him the chance to be as prosperous as he had always planned to be. He had built up his reputation, established a mind for business, invested profits, and bought and sold houses. He raised millions in capital for a start-up company. He bought his dream house and developed life-long friendships while still traveling home often enough to be the favorite uncle. He considered himself successful. But by 2008, his success, money, and hope for a good life in Jackson was slipping away. The pain from his previous life still remained.

Even now Michael felt like he was outside of his front door again, wondering why his key didn't work. He had been running his whole life. What was he chasing? Why couldn't God just let him catch it for once? These questions taunted him. He was supposed to rest, relax, mend. Yet even as he lay there, half-conscious, he considered what he needed to change. Something had gone wrong, and he was determined to make it right.

He woke up with a start.

"I didn't realize you were sleeping," Dawn said, folding a clean t-shirt. "You were talking quite a bit to yourself when I came in."

Michael struggled to sit up and watch as Dawn put clothes in different drawers. The first time he had seen her, her liveliness, her confidence had stolen his attention. He remembered feeling curious about her. *I didn't know how I didn't know her. I knew everyone in Jackson.*

She hadn't been too impressed by him, he knew that much. She made it known with her faint, polite smiles and slow nods as her eyes looked past him around the room. Now he was with her, they belonged to each other, and she was folding his laundry while he struggled to move around the house. When Michael asked her to marry him, he had left clues for her around town that led her to all of their special places and ended with the proposal at the church. Now she was forced to guide him around the house and the vacant places of his mind where the answers should be.

He was embarrassed, perhaps even ashamed. "I don't know what to do, Dawn."

"What do you mean?" she asked playfully though she knew where he was going with his words.

"I don't know what's going to happen from here...with us, with the girls, with our lives. I don't think I can fix it."

"Yeah," Dawn said. "I guess God's got you now that you are down."

"What is that supposed to mean?" he asked, his muscles tightening.

Dawn stopped working and sat down on the bed next to him. She chose her words carefully. "I mean that you can't do anything. You just need to let go."

"Let go of what?" he asked though both of them knew what she meant and neither voiced an answer. "I can't," Michael said finally.

"You can."

"All right. I can. Easy as that," Michael replied in frustration.

Dawn gave him a sarcastic smile, stood up, shoved a drawer shut loudly, and walked out of the room.

Michael barely noticed. He knew she was right.

"Okay, God," he began. "You take this. You fix this. I should know from how much You've fixed already." The thought was humbling. He felt helpless. After all that God had done to save him, why was he still so stubborn? So angry?

```
AUGUST 10, 2012

PRUETT RESIDENCE,
PINE DRIVE
6:34 MT
```

Michael walked slowly down his driveway with Willie, his dog, in tow. A sliver of early morning sun cast a pale glow on the street. The trees stood tall, their silent shadows almost whispering from the breeze that shook their statuesque forms.

The past two weeks had been gruesome—his body ached severely, he had lost his voice at one point, he wasn't fully aware mentally, and he was pretty much confined to his house. Although he had been told to strictly stay in bed except for occasional walks and exercise like he was getting now, he couldn't help but check in with work. The previous four years had been so difficult financially, and now being practically bed-ridden, he did not know how his real-estate efforts would fare. On top of catching up on all of his work emails, his inbox had also been filled with dozens of "get well" messages, prayers, and comforting words from family, friends, and colleagues. While it was great to know that so many people cared about him, there was nothing in any of the messages that relieved his growing anxiety about his business.

Then there was Dawn. He knew it was providential that she had already been on sabbatical when the accident occurred, but whether it was a fair assessment or not, he also knew that in his current condition he was causing her a lot of stress.

Pastor Mike had visited the day before, probably more for Dawn than for him. Either way, Michael was glad to see he had returned to check in with the Pruett household. Walking quietly into his living room, he had overheard Dawn relaying his progress to Mike.

"He'll get there," Pastor Mike had said comfortingly.

He'll get there. Michael's demeanor deflated. Wherever he needed to be, he obviously wasn't there yet. As illogical as he knew it was, Michael was ashamed and had been since the beginning of his recovery. His wife was trying to find solace in Pastor Mike's comforting words because *he* couldn't comfort her.

"You know what I think," Mike had said casually. "Michael's still relying on *Michael* to see this thing through."

Catapulted suddenly out of his degrading thoughts about Pastor Mike's visit, Michael lifted his head. Deehan's mini cooper was turning up into his driveway. A smile crept onto Michael's face. *A welcome distraction,* he thought.

When Deehan stepped out of his small vehicle, he looked like a giant in comparison. His hair was messy, as if to mark the early hour. Teddy, his rather large yet kind-hearted mutt, jumped out after him and stretched. Willie was suddenly attentive and ran up to greet his canine friend. Glancing down the driveway at Michael, Deehan squinted against the early sunlight.

Michael lumbered toward him, still caught in thought.

"Hey, buddy!" Deehan called out.

Michael snapped out of his thoughts completely and stared at him with a grin. "Hey man. Sorry. I'm still a little spacey."

Sauntering toward one another, the two men embraced. "I guess I'll forgive you. I think after you almost die you get like six to eight months where you can do or say whatever you want. People will still feel sorry for you. Milk it."

Michael's dismal expression faded almost instantly. "You're right," he abdicated, "but please inform my wife of that rule."

After they greeted Dawn, she urged the two friends to go sit outside and talk. "I've had my time with Deehan the past month. Your turn."

"What am I, a prison sentence?" Deehan joked.

"I said, 'had my time,' not 'done my time,'" Dawn chided.

As the two men walked outside, Dawn moved a pillow into Michael's chair and then helped him sit down into a comfortable position. Michael thanked her, slightly self-conscious about needing her assistance just to sit.

"So, Michael," Deehan teased. "Everything's back to normal, I guess."

"I know, I know," Michael laughed. "I hope so soon." Then he added, "I think I need to start referring to my life as 'pre' and 'post-accident.'"

"I'll hold you to it!" Deehan chuckled, and then stated more seriously, "Really though, you look two-hundred percent better."

Michael nodded. "That's not hard to do. I had staples on my scalp."

"Yeah, but I don't just mean physically."

"Well," Michael started to respond but only ended with a heavy exhale and carefully scratched the stitches on the back of his neck.

"You know it's okay to just be," Deehan stated, leaning forward. "Don't you?"

"I know."

"Then why do you seem embarrassed by it?"

"Since when did you become my spiritual guru?" Michael teased.

Deehan's complexion turned ruddy. "I've just had a lot of time to think through this whole experience. And you know what? I think there's something bigger going on here than you've admitted."

Michael analyzed Deehan's expression and realized his sincerity. "No, seriously...I don't know why I'm embarrassed," he noted, looking down at his hands and then off into the trees. He felt like a Catholic boy at confession. "I guess I just want to be able to take care of my family, not need my family to take care of me."

"Michael, you were hit by a truck. I'll say that again. You were hit by a *truck*."

Michael grinned. "I know it doesn't make sense."

"I'm just grateful I can sit here and talk to you. For a minute there I didn't know if that was ever going to happen again."

Deehan stared at his friend and then, somewhat sheepishly, looked away. "I'm still deeply hurt about several losses in my life, more than I realized. Of course it mainly has to do with Kristen. This ordeal with you has made me recognize that the pain of losing her will never go away. It'll ebb and flow for the rest of my life. If you hadn't survived the crash, I could have remained...bitter. It would've been a major challenge for me on many levels."

Michael looked at Deehan, waiting for him to explain, but he didn't.

"Look," Deehan finally said. "I didn't come here to talk about me, but I will tell you that I've seen the impossible happen to you, and I believe it's for good reason. Just don't waste whatever it is you are supposed to learn from this. You see your scars as something bad that happened to you, and it was. But I look at your scars, and I feel like freaking Doubting Thomas. Your scars are right here in front of me…and they mean something."

"And I guess I'm Jesus in that scenario," Michael offered impassively.

"Well," Deehan smirked. "Yeah, okay. I guess you get to be Jesus."

The two men stared at each other expectantly.

"You know, I have a lot of respect for you, Michael," Deehan continued. "You are a hard worker and in some ways it has paid off for you. Even though I'm not a believer in the American Dream, you are a pretty good picture of it, for all its pros and cons. But the idea that if you just work hard enough, you'll arrive—it isn't necessarily true."

Everything Michael had ever been taught, everything he had heard about great leaders, about success, was linked to determination and hard work. "I'm not sure I know where this is coming from," he said sharply. Deehan was beginning to sound a lot like the conviction he had felt the past few years but had been too proud to pay attention to.

Deehan squinted his eyes again to see Michael's face without the glare from the sun. "You've been going hard after success most of your life. I have too. I'm not judging you for God's sake. But we both say we believe in grace and salvation and at the same time, we still believe that success is pretty much everything."

Michael was agitated, physically and emotionally. He wasn't in the mood to get serious. Couldn't he just brood a little, alone? He knew that the idea that he could control the outcome if he just worked hard enough was always at war with grace. He could quote more scriptures than Deehan on God's grace being "perfect in weakness," but he had avoided that as best as he could. Now he actually felt weak. A little unwillingly, Michael listened to Deehan and let his words go past the surface of his mind. He knew what his friend was saying was true.

"Just think about it. Let's just get over the *stepdaughters* label— your *daughters* told you they loved you for the first time when you were basically unconscious in a hospital bed. You didn't do anything to fix that. It was fixed without your help or even your permission."

Michael felt his vision blur with tears, but restrained himself. The heart of Deehan's words brought truth, which gave him a feeling he had not experienced since long before the accident.

"Come on, man. You should have died. Did you do anything about that? I mean, you couldn't even pray about it. I saw so much happen for you when you weren't even really there. You are walking. You are making sense when you talk, which is a miracle. God did something for you, for all of us."

Michael couldn't respond. Why would God care enough to look past all of his mistakes, his stubbornness with Dawn, his blunders with his girls, his pride over money? Why would God, for some inexplicable reason, give him another chance? Not everyone got one.

"I've got to head out to work," Deehan said, rising from his chair. He reached over and very cautiously tousled Michael's matted hair. "Glad you took a shower this morning." He extended his hand.

"Thanks for coming by," Michael said with a puzzled brow, but then reached over to grasp Deehan's hand.

"I'm going to say goodbye to Dawn. Do you need anything?"

Michael shook his head. "I'm good. I'm going to sit out here for a minute. Fresh air."

Deehan gave him a knowing look and then ambled inside.

Michael turned his attention to his surroundings. Jackson Hole still lay mostly quiet below, but he knew many young people would already be hiking or fitting in some other adventure before work. It was still within the short months of summer. A slight breeze jostled the pine leaves, creating an enigmatic effect.

Just then, Willie came to sit beside him and looked up at him in earnest.

Michael reached out slowly to pat him, calling him by his familiar nickname, "Haaaandsome dog."

For all the natural beauty around him, his mind was dominated by his best friend's words. In truth he was bothered by them—and Dawn's words, and Pastor Mike's words—and he sat there in silence. Why did the whole conversation make him feel so uncomfortable?

"Do you have an opinion to share?" he asked Willie.

Willie panted and whined.

Michael knew from his earliest years that if he wanted something, he'd have to work for it. He wasn't going to be given an easy pass to fulfill his goals. His mother and father had taught him that he wasn't better than anyone else or the task put before him. He worked every summer of his teenage years.

This work ethic applied just as much to his idea of Christianity as it did to business. He remembered the pivotal moment in his childhood at Kanakuk. There as a young boy he heard about God and Jesus and the devil. He had become impassioned to stand up for God during what some Christians deemed "The Last Days." He had promised to cut off his arm rather than be imprinted with the "Mark of the Beast." There was a battle between good and evil, and with those experiences at such a young age, how could he not want to do something for God? Michael knew he could become a good man; he could do great things. He could share his faith and excel in school; he could make a lot of money without coming under its power and charm. He could make his way in the world and be a responsible member of society. God rewarded good decisions; there were consequences for bad ones. He believed he had what it took, and he had decided he would not fail.

After Michael's dad, Don, finished his second Army tour, he joined a surgical practice with his father and another surgeon. Michael wanted to continue the legacy. He knew there was no career more perfect than being a doctor to satisfy his need for financial success and contribution to society. He started college as a pre-med major, but quickly felt that committing to such a long path of training before knowing if he even had the passion or skill for it was too risky. He turned his attention elsewhere, eventually getting a Bachelor of Arts in Business and Economics at Vanderbilt. From the beginning of his profession in the field, everything seemed to be shaping up nicely for him. He was scouted for a job at Anderson Consulting in Nashville, and the offer—$25,000 a year with the chance to gain the skills and necessary connections to one day start his own business—lured him.

He had embarked on his path brimming with optimism. His risk had paid off. He was going to create a place in this world near the top, and he was going to do it with ease. He married his high school sweetheart and aimed to give her the life he knew they both deserved. In his early twenties, Michael was proud of himself and his accomplishments. He believed things could only go up from there, yet in the back of his mind was a simple question that kept him awake at night: *What if this isn't 'it'?*

He never wanted to answer the question, and it wasn't too long after this that he didn't have to. The worst happened. His career didn't go as planned, his sister-in-law died, and his wife served him divorce papers. Even though everything he had built was slipping away, he still believed it was his responsibility to fix. If it had been God's voice in the back of Michael's mind asking for his trust, then Michael had given his answer. *I've got this*, he would say, shifting from one venture to the next, picking up the pieces of his life, and moving them to Jackson.

Sitting outside and watching the wind blow through the trees, Michael heard that same voice call to him, the one he had always brushed aside. He had answered it many times before, "I get it, okay? I'll get back on track. Just let this season be over."

This time was different. He was beyond the point of questions. He no longer needed to know "Why?" or "What if?" and frankly, he was tired. Tired of running from failure or running toward success. Tired of wondering where he had gone wrong. Tired of carrying the weight of being a good man, a good Christian, a good son, a good husband. He knew he had to make a decision, and he was finally allowing himself to be weak enough to sit down on the side of the road he had been running on so long and actually make it.

"I lived through it," he said quietly. "I lived through it well before my accident. I'm tired, God. I don't think I can figure it out anymore. I don't think I want to. Please...rebuild my life."

Suddenly Michael knew what he had been running toward, and it was more than success. It was worthiness. He looked up at the sky.

I think I really get it this time.

At that, Michael fully felt his brokenness. His body had been thrown off course. His mind, for a time, had been also. Now he was being asked to let go of his strong-as-iron will. Michael covered his eyes with his hands and cried tears that brought relief, even healing. Losing control—*that* was his worst fear, and that fear had already been realized many times over. Somehow and for some reason, Michael's life had been spared. He had been given a gift by God, and it wasn't just his life or his ability to walk.

When Michael went inside, he found his wife and gently embraced her. After a moment of silence, he finally spoke. "I think I can try to do what you said earlier. I think I'm ready to let go."

Dawn let Michael hold her, and they stood there together without saying a word.

Michael lay in bed as instructed by his wife and checked his email, mostly out of boredom and restlessness. He was used to this daily routine now, spending the mornings on the porch and the afternoons in bed before dinner. As he perused the inbox, his eye caught an email from his colleague, Richard Lewis. He read Richard's letter in disbelief. Then he read it again.

In Michael's absence, Richard, with the help of his wife Edie and a few others, had taken over his pending sales and accounts in escrow. If Michael had known this, he would have been nervous, assuming that Richard—one of his main rivals at work—would have used this to his advantage. That Richard had even shown up at the hospital after the accident was surprise enough for Michael to hear, but the information Richard shared in this email left Michael astounded.

"Three closings?" Michael asked in disbelief. "In one day?"

What Michael was reading was what he had always hoped for, but never actually got. Being a real estate agent in Jackson Hole, of all places in the U.S., could be lucrative if one deal per year was secured. Michael had not closed a major deal in four years. Now Richard, who focused more on larger ranch parcels rather than local commercial real estate, was informing him that he had secured *three* on Michael's behalf.

Dawn walked into the bedroom just as Michael became fully aware of their financial situation. "Dawn," he said, the excitement building in his voice. "I just had three closings."

"That's great, honey," she replied, her attention focused on the mess that Michael's eating, drinking, and sleeping had left in their bedroom.

"No," Michael commanded her attention. "You don't understand."

Dawn turned to face him with a sheepish look on her face and sat down beside him. "All right, I'm focused," she mused, smirking at him.

"I've never had three closings so close together throughout my entire career, let alone in the same day! The commission from these sales will provide..." Michael's voice cracked. He shook his head and tried to speak again. "This will provide for us and the girls for several *years*."

Dawn looked confused and then, realizing what he was attempting to tell her, asked, "How is that even possible?"

"Richard helped close three deals for me," Michael said, quickly reading through the email again to be sure.

"Richard took over for you?" Dawn summarized, "and now—"

"Now we have enough money to cover...*everything*," Michael interrupted.

"Okay, you mean all the...." her voice quieted, as the full weight of their upswing hit her. "Oh my God!" she said, embracing Michael.

"I know!" Michael laughed while he held her.

Dawn pushed away from him to look into his face once again, "God has been good to us, Michael."

"*That*, my love, is an understatement."

Willie's yelp drew his attention. Michael leaned down to scratch the fur behind Willie's ears. How was it possible that Richard would want to be there for him after everything they'd been through? Michael picked up the phone and called his office. One of the greatest blessings in his life had come from one of his greatest competitors.

Point taken, he thought, waiting for a voice on the other end of the line.

When Richard finally answered, he avoided the subject entirely. "Michael! What are you doing? You're not supposed to be calling in."

Michael hesitated at first before getting to the heart of it. "Richard... I...just got your email."

Richard quieted on the other end.

"I can't believe...I don't think 'thank you' is enough."

"Michael, please, it was—"

"No. You are a good man. You have outdone any kindness that I would have shown you. I don't know what else to say except that I am blessed by your friendship and your actions." Something terrible and tragic had brought them together, and now good was stemming from it. Michael knew the colossal gift Richard's actions would bring to his personal life.

"That's not all of it," Richard eagerly answered, his voice effusing satisfaction. "You had another closing go through after I sent you that email."

"What?" Michael shook his head in amazement and stared at Dawn. "That makes four closings," he mouthed to her. *That is impossible*, he told himself.

Michael cleared his throat. He didn't want to break down in front of his former rival. "Richard—I, I don't know what to say."

"You don't need to say anything. I've got the paperwork handled, and I'll brief you about everything when you're back. I just didn't want you to worry about medical bills, you know?"

It took a few moments before Michael could speak clearly. "Okay, Richard. Again, thank you." He hung up the phone. "God, I can't believe it," he said aloud, choking up. "I am amazed by this kindness." In total, the sales amounted to over $3,000,000.

Only one month had passed since the day he dropped Dawn off prior to racing down the hill into the center of Jackson Hole. Since that time too many "coincidences" had taken place for Michael not to recognize the work of Providence. If Dawn had still been on the back of his bike, she wouldn't have survived. First responders were at the scene of the accident because they were having dinner after work across the street. The ambulance that arrived first on scene had been a block away at a gas station. When Dawn heard its siren, she knew it was Michael, as if already prepared for the news. Her recent sabbatical allowed her the freedom to be with him through the entire process. Despite Michael's traumatized body, his tumultuous flailing hadn't caused further damage to his spine. He received care by the EMT team that not only kept him alive, but also enabled him to walk again. He survived a major transfer from Saint John's to the University of Salt Lake City's hospital. One of the best neurosurgeons in the country happened to be free to perform the surgery. His stepdaughters expressed their love toward him for the first time and now saw him differently. He regained his mental capacities within ten days and was on his way to full recovery without long-term effects. In the meantime, his colleague helped make him a millionaire overnight.

Michael felt like he was in a dream, but this time a good one. He had always believed it was up to him to be good enough, to be successful. He had never imagined that at his worst and weakest, his life could go in such a dramatically positive direction. In the midst of a wreck, his life had been restored. So much had been overcome, and none of it had occurred because of his effort. It had all happened outside of his control.

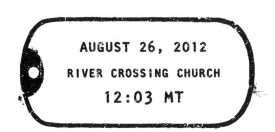

AUGUST 26, 2012
RIVER CROSSING CHURCH
12:03 MT

That next Sunday, Michael and Dawn attended church as normal. After the service was over and the crowd of friends and acquaintances began to clear out, Michael pulled Pastor Mike aside to discuss all that he had been contemplating.

Pastor Mike agreed with his conclusions. "I think it's a new day for you, Michael. The start of a whole new life."

The phrase struck Michael. He had been raised in a religious home and even been a Christian from a young age. Yet it wasn't until now, decades later, that he understood what it felt like to live out that overused, almost cliché phrase—to be *born again*. Now the words were the only way to accurately capture it. The need to get "there," that unclear, elusive place, was gone. He had let go of the reins, or at least he didn't hold onto them so tightly anymore. *A whole new life.*

As Dawn gathered their things to leave, Michael watched her, admiring her strength and beauty and feeling grateful that he was even able to be there. She could just as easily have had to prepare a funeral in this same building.

"I guess it's strange to imagine what to do now," Michael confessed.

Pastor Mike laughed. "Now you get to *live*. And maybe stop trying so hard."

His words rested on Michael. Even through his spiritual encounters, he had always relied on himself, initiated and done the "right" thing. He hated to fail and believed that if he didn't come through for himself he couldn't expect anyone else to come through for him. Now, he could finally trust God to work through him by simply being himself. No more, "I have to fix this myself," mentality. He wouldn't have to try, he could just be.

"Just give me a minute," Michael requested of Dawn. She nodded and walked toward the entrance without him.

Everyone else had left the sanctuary. Michael looked up toward the front of the church. The late summer sun filtered through the oversized window behind the stage. He noticed the shape of the cross that was hewn into the wooden altar and sighed in peace. This was where he had come back to faith after years of wandering. This was where he had proposed to Dawn. This was a place he hoped to have many more experiences for the rest of his life—because he was alive. He had survived, and he knew that he could never go back to the way things were. Michael's life had already changed so much, and he was thankful. His recovery was God's victory, not his. He could not claim it as his effort, his intelligence, or his diligence.

He choked on his own tears as they began to fall. How did he deserve such love and attention? He knew that grace meant he didn't deserve it—

that was the whole point. It was a gift. In that moment, he could feel that grace almost tangibly. He wanted others to experience the comfort, the safety, of being seen and loved. Michael wanted to love Dawn and the girls unconditionally, perfectly without fear. Because God loved him just as he was, he had the ability to love them in that same way.

"You healed me," Michael said. "You put me back together."

Nothing he could have done or could do now would ever merit or explain God's love. He felt utterly humbled. After a few minutes, he wiped his face clean with his hands and turned to leave. Dawn was waiting for him by the double wooden doors at the front entrance.

When she witnessed the tears on his face, she asked with a smile, "Michael, what happened to you?"

Michael looked up into the sky in amusement as they walked through the church doors. "I don't know what this is." Then he felt himself begin to laugh—a deep and joyful laugh. "I am alive and well! If I become one of those emotional yuppies, so be it." For the first time since the accident Michael knew what kind of life he wanted to live—a full one, one that extended beyond himself and his own capabilities.

As they started toward cars in the parking lot, Michael stopped, confused.

"I thought we parked over here," he said in bewilderment, glancing around.

Dawn snickered. "Some things don't change, I guess."

Michael smiled. "Okay, okay. Cut me some slack," he said. "I got hit by a truck."

THE MEDICAL STORY

BY MEIC H. SCHMIDT, MD, MBA
WRITTEN ON OCTOBER 28, 2014

Professor Meic H. Schmidt, MD, MBA, is a German-American neurosurgeon with specialized expertise in neuro-oncology and spine surgery. His main clinical focus is management of patients with tumors and injuries to the spine and spinal cord.

Dr. Schmidt is the Vice Chair for Clinical Affairs in the Department of Neurosurgery at the University of Utah. He is a tenured Professor of Neurosurgery and Orthopaedics and holds the Ronald I. Apfelbaum, MD, Endowed Chair in Spine Surgery. Dr. Schmidt co-directs the Brain, Spine, and Skull Base Cancer Program at the Huntsman Cancer Institute and serves as Director of the Spinal Oncology Service. He is also the Chief Value Officer at University Hospital for the Neurosurgery Service Line.

He received his bachelor's degree in Psychology from the University of Utah. He went on to obtain his MD with Honors in Research in Photodynamic Therapy and completed a neurosurgical residency at the

Medical College of Wisconsin. Dr. Schmidt was awarded funding from the National Institutes of Health for training at the University of California, San Francisco, where he completed back-to-back fellowships in Neuro-oncology and Spinal Surgery at the UCSF Brain Tumor Research Center and the Department of Neurological Surgery. More recently, Dr. Schmidt completed the Executive MBA at the David Eccles School of Business at the University of Utah.

Dr. Schmidt has been married to his wife, Wendy, for over twenty-five years. They have four successful children, Eric, Katarina, Alexandra, and Albert.

As I reflect on how Michael Pruett experienced his trauma, hospitalization, and treatment, I find it interesting that his story offers a completely different point of view from my own as the treating physician. His story is truly remarkable, and I will summarize his medical history from a physician's perspective.

Mr. Michael Pruett was admitted under the name Trauma Kelp (his real name was not known to us at that time) on 07/16/2012 to the Neurosurgery Service at the University of Utah Hospital. Earlier in the day, I received a phone call from Saint John's in Jackson Hole. A spine surgeon had reviewed Mr. Pruett's images and informed me about his case. Mr. Pruett had suffered a grave fracture dislocation between the cervical and thoracic parts of his spine. The degree of separation was severe and nearly complete, meaning that his spinal cord was practically detached from his spinal column. The medical term for his kind of injury is a cervicothoracic fracture dislocation (spondyloptosis). **SEE FIGURE 1.**

The physician in Jackson Hole requested a transfer to our hospital

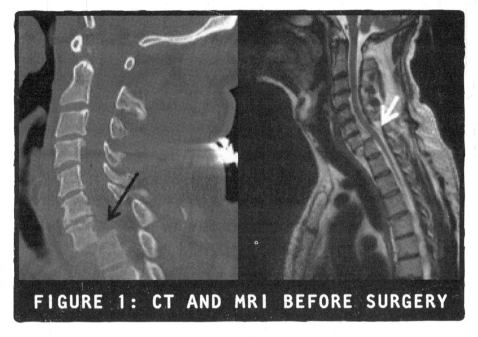

FIGURE 1: CT AND MRI BEFORE SURGERY

Figure 1: (Left) Computer tomogram (CT) and (right) magnetic resonance imaging (MRI) scans both represent side views of Michael Pruett's neck. The CT scan shows the severe step off between the 7th cervical spine bone and the 1st thoracic spine bone (fracture dislocation). The MRI shows the spinal cord "draped" and stretched over the step off from the fracture.

because of the challenge that this particular injury poses. Most patients with this degree of fracture dislocation have a spinal cord injury with complete separation. In these cases a patient is already paralyzed, and reduction of the spine (which restores the fracture to its correct alignment) can be achieved easily and without risk because the injury is not able to be reversed. In Mr. Pruett's case, the miracle that he remained largely neurologically intact after his accident actually made the procedure of aligning the spine and fixing it risky since the surgical process itself could have caused further injury to his spinal cord.

In addition to his severe cervical spine fracture, Mr. Pruett also sustained other injuries, most significantly a large head injury. **SEE FIGURE 2.** This extracranial injury consisted of a scalp injury that resulted in a large hematoma (blood clot) outside of the skull. In addition, he also suffered injuries to his brain and the surroundings of his brain inside of the skull, including hematomas, or small bruises inside of his brain, and also a subdural hematoma between the skull and his brain.

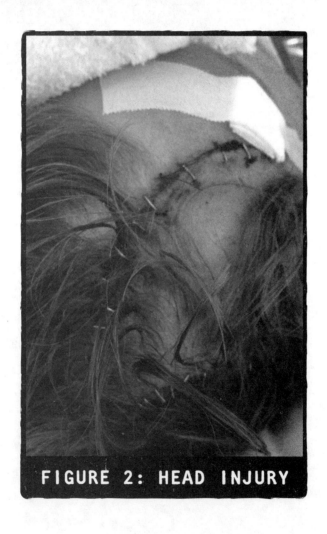

FIGURE 2: HEAD INJURY

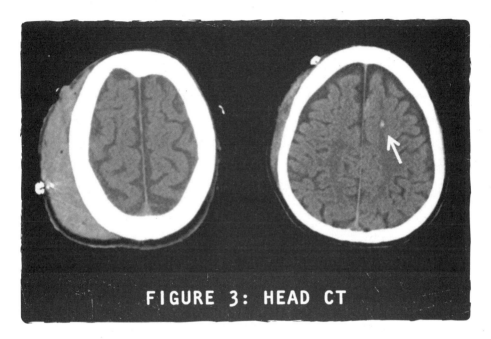

FIGURE 3: HEAD CT

Figure 3: CT images of Michael Pruett's head. The image on the left shows a large blood clot outside of the skull from his extensive scalp injury. The image on the right shows a small bleed in the brain itself that can indicate severe brain injury.

SEE FIGURE 3. This combination of head injury and severe spine fracture is common and makes the assessment of a patient difficult because we usually rely on the patient's verbal report of his symptoms like numbness, tingling, and weakness. With a severe head injury, the patient may not be able to assess his symptoms accurately. Overall, however, Mr. Pruett was completely neurologically intact within the limitations of his head injury, which was phenomenal.

After assessing Mr. Pruett, we thought that it was best to attempt to realign the spine while he was concious even though his mental status was foggy. This is a time-honored method of reducing the spinal fracture, and because the patient is awake during that part of the procedure, he is able to report if he develops new symptoms that could indicate potential spinal cord damage from the realignment. The benefit obtained from this patient perspective makes it worthwhile.

The way this realignment procedure is conducted is by putting small screws into the patient's head and attaching them to a ring through which we then hang weights to create traction so the fracture can be realigned. The amount of weight needed to reduce a fracture at the cervicothoracic junction can be quite large. In particular, Mr. Pruett's muscular build made a reduction such as this difficult. Plus, Mr. Pruett's head injury involved hematomas, which can sometimes mask skull fractures on CT scans and can make the placement of screws in the skull for traction difficult. Despite all these circumstances, we felt we should at least try to align his spine in this very safe method. Unfortunately, this method was not successful in reducing Mr. Pruett's spine, and we were back in the position of needing to realign and fix the spine with the patient asleep (under anesthesia) where he cannot report his neurological symptoms should they get worse during realignment. The safest way to do the surgery is in three stages, so on 07/16/2012, Mr. Pruett underwent a three-stage surgery. The surgery was very extensive and labor-intensive and took eight hours to complete.

A situation such as this is always complicated, and to explain these circumstances to a family that is in shock from trauma can be quite challenging. It is remarkable how Mr. Pruett's family, in particular his wife Dawn, took the news and put their trust in our team to perform this difficult surgery.

In the first stage of the procedure, Mr. Pruett underwent a surgery with an incision through the front of his neck. The dislocated vertebral body at C7 including the adjacent discs was removed during this process. This decompressed the spinal cord, and we were also able to evacuate hematomas and disc fragments that were compressing his spinal cord. At this point, although the spinal cord was decompressed, the spine was not yet realigned, but we closed the wound and turned the patient on his belly. We then began the second part of the procedure, which exposes the back of the spine. During this part, we placed screws into the vertebral

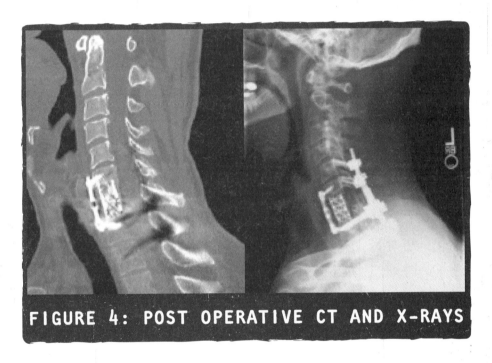

FIGURE 4: POST OPERATIVE CT AND X-RAYS

Figure 4: The left panel shows a post-surgical CT from a side view. Compared with the images in Figure 1, the spine is realigned. The 7th cervical bone has been replaced with a titanium cage that was attached with a plate to the spine. The X-ray on the right also demonstrates near-perfect alignment and the screws and rods that were placed from the back to secure the spinal alignment.

bodies above and below the fracture site. Due to the pedicle screws, the fracture was then reduced, which meant the spine was realigned. This can be done fairly safely because the anterior part of the spine was already decompressed and there was nothing preventing the spine from realigning.

Once the spine was reduced (brought into the correct position), we connected all the screws with rods to stabilize the spine. At this point, there was still a large defect in front from the decompression, or where the C7 vertebra was removed. The patient was once again flipped carefully onto his back, and the incision from the first surgery was reopened. Then, the vertebral body that had been removed was replaced with a titanium metal cage. We then secured it to the spine with a plate to complete the procedure. **SEE FIGURE 4.**

Mr. Pruett awoke very well after the surgery and remained neurologically intact. He then completed his stay in the intensive care unit and his subsequent rehabilitation. **SEE FIGURE 5.**

Now, almost three years since the accident, Mr. Pruett is doing well, and has returned to work. Only minimal symptoms as a result of his injury, hospitalization, and treatment remain.

His accident and the fact that he remained neurologically intact after such severe trauma is truly remarkable. The research literature for such rare fractures indicates that it is very unusual for people to remain neurologically intact without spinal cord injury. Equally remarkable is that with modern medical care, spine surgery, and team work, such an injury can be fixed in a safe manner.

Personally speaking, one of the most rewarding experiences as a physician is to see patients like Mr. Pruett recover from a life-

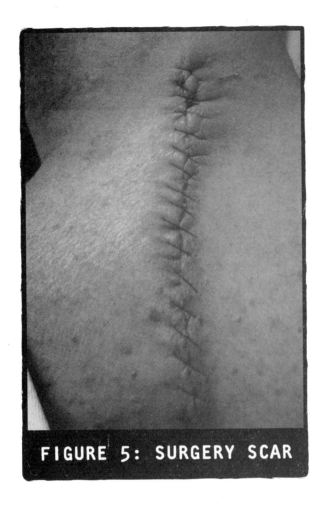

FIGURE 5: SURGERY SCAR

threatening event such as his and return to a truly fulfilling life. In the field of neurosurgery, it is uncommon to experience this other end of the spectrum because patients typically die from such severe injuries or remain permanently paralyzed.

It is the successful recovery of patients like Mr. Pruett that helps us maintain the motivation to stay in this most rewarding profession.

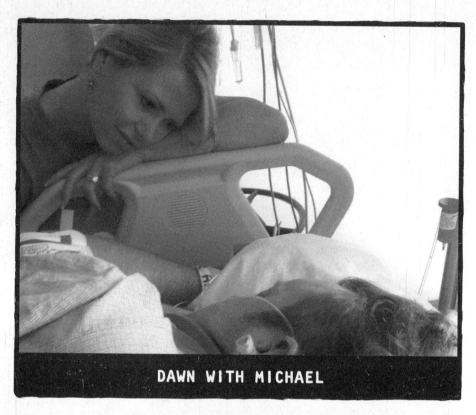

DAWN WITH MICHAEL

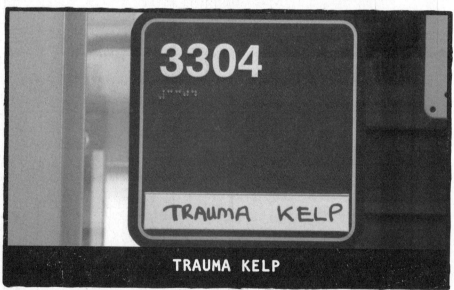

3304

TRAUMA KELP

TRAUMA KELP

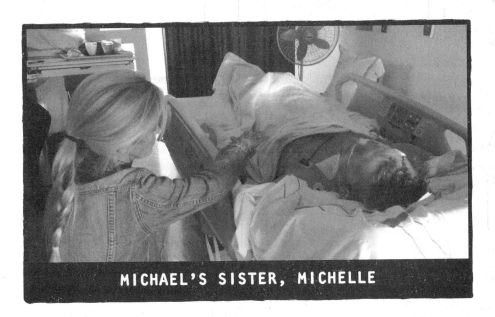

MICHAEL'S SISTER, MICHELLE

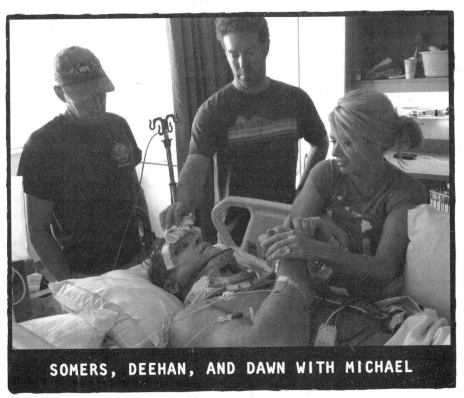

SOMERS, DEEHAN, AND DAWN WITH MICHAEL

AFTERWORD

The records indicate that I was not at fault in the accident. While I was recovering, I had a lot of time to think and question why this happened...why me? Why did I survive? Is there a lesson to be learned through this, or is it just one of life's curve balls that happens to get thrown at whomever is in the way?

I tried to understand why I felt guilty that I fully recovered from my accident without long-term injury when it could have been much worse. Since that fateful day—July 15, 2012, people stop me in the grocery store, at my office, or walking in town. They remember my accident and are curious how I survived. Remarkably, they also often share their own stories of pain. Sometimes it's something that has happened to them personally; sometimes it's a loved one. I listen to their stories of suffering on a daily basis. Some of these situations turn out for the better in the end, but on some occasions, regrettably they don't.

During these moments, I realize my story is small in comparison to others. Yet it has become clear to me that I should share my story, not just of the accident but also more importantly of God's great love that I have come to understand more fully through this experience. The God of Creation loves me so much that He is involved in the details of my life. I believe that miracles are real and still occur today, but I also believe it is the healing of hearts that interests Him most. He has shown me that I need to be completely committed to Him, trusting in Him and His Word, not out of obligation, but from a heart of thankfulness for what He has done for me. He has asked me to be "all in," and I am.

God loves His people. Whether it is cancer, an accident, tragedy, loss of a loved one, sickness, a financial crisis, or other source of distress, He is there in the midst of it. He is a loving Father. In my case, I could not avoid the pain. He did not remove it. He did, however, provide me with love, comfort, and peace to help me overcome it. Even though others may not be able to relate to my accident and physical pain, they can relate to the fear, anger, doubt, stress, and agony I experienced.

In a time when I was younger and questioning my faith, my father sent me a simple letter that said, "God has not changed. He is the same as He has always been." I have kept that card in my wallet ever since. It is worn and almost torn in half, but that note means so much to me. Through this event in my life, the meaning of it has become even more real and has a much broader meaning to me. He truly is the same God that Abraham, Isaac, and Jacob served. He remains unchanged. His deep, consistent love remains unchanged. He still performs miracles today. He still parts seas, raises men from the dead, turns water into wine, provides for the needs of His children, and heals people physically. So many of us believe that not only has God changed, but that we have advanced beyond foolish, ancient knowledge and come so far in our modern lives and societies. But we haven't changed either. We are the same lost, broken men and women, searching to fill a void in our lives that can only be filled by the love of Christ. I hope that my story leads you to find Him and His great love.

MICHAEL PRUETT

Michael Pruett is a prominent residential and commercial real estate broker at Jackson Hole Real Estate Associates in Wyoming. Originally from St. Louis, Missouri, Michael graduated from Vanderbilt University in Nashville, Tennessee. He started his career as a small business consultant with Accenture, which exposed him to all aspects of business and grounded him in finance and administration. He has since expanded into co-founding and later selling OneWest.net, at one time the largest ISP in the Intermountain West, and into developing and selling residential property. He has served on several local boards including the Community Safety Network and the Town of Jackson Planning Commission.

He is married to Dawn Paxton-Pruett and is dedicated to his three stepdaughters, his extended family in St. Louis, and his friends and community in Jackson Hole. After his near-death experience as told in *The Hard Road*, Michael gained even greater fervor for his religious beliefs and now desires to share his message of hope with others.

VANESSA JOY CHANDLER

Vanessa Joy Chandler began her career in the field of publishing in 2004 as a freelance creative writer and editor. Since that time, she has built her platform through editing for entities such as ABC-CLIO educational publishers, Book of Hope, Hope Education, HigherLife Development Services, Destiny Image Publishers, Regal/Gospel Light Publishing, and articles in *Charisma* and *CALLED* magazines. She has been recognized and won awards for her pursuits in leadership, music, teaching, and writing. Vanessa holds a Bachelor of Arts in Literature, certified credentials in English and Social Science, and a Top Gun achievement award in Frank Consulting's Business Bootcamp. In the past six years, Vanessa has played a significant role in three start-up companies, ghostwritten four books including *Prosperity with Purpose* by Mike Frank and *The Hard Road* by Michael S. Pruett, and acted as a publishing consultant and manager of six book projects through her company Red Arrow Media including the top-selling *Keep Your Love On!*, which is currently being translated and distributed in 17 nations.

ACKNOWLEDGEMENTS

To my wife, Dawn: What would I do without your love in my life? I love the woman that you are—your strength, composure, intelligence and your ability to touch others. You are a great mother, a loving wife, and a true friend. Your heart grows bigger, stronger, and softer toward God each year. You make me want to be a better man. I am honored and humbled to be your husband. I love you madly.

To Chris (Keeks) and Michelle, my brother and sister: Thank you for your unwavering commitment to your faith, family, and me. It is incredible to go through life knowing that you believe in me no matter what. I could not ask for a better brother and sister or better examples for my life.

To Mom and Dad: Thank you for your constant love for me, Michelle, and Chris. You have taught us much in life through your example. You have taught me that love is so much more than words; it is also sacrifice and devotion and pouring your life into another, many times an action and not always a feeling. I love you both.

To my daughters, Jade, Paige, and Karsen: Thank you for loving and accepting me, and thank you for participating in this book. It takes strength and courage to be open, honest, and vulnerable. I love you, and I am proud of who you are today and the women you are becoming.

To Matty Deehan and Matt Somers: Thank you for being so loyal. You have taught me what it means to be dedicated and committed. I hope I can be half the friend to you as you both are to me.

To my friends who gave of their time and prayer: Dan and Christina

Feuz, Richard and Edie Lewis, Nathan and Emily Ver Berg, and Pastor Mike Atkins. Your constant prayers were heard! Your dedication and commitment to my family and me is beyond words.

To everyone at Red Arrow Media, Vanessa Chandler, Sarah Harris, Megan Cotton, and Jennifer Westbrook: What a talented and professional group! Special thanks to Vanessa Chandler—without your consistent dedication to this project, your talents and writing skills, none of this would have been possible. You saw the vision from the beginning, brought each person's perspective and experience to life, and helped share this miraculous event.

To David Noroña at Cuentista Productions: Your vision, combined with your production talents and skills, are invaluable and surpass the size and scope of this project. Thank you for making the promotional video such a quality production and for recognizing the opportunity to touch people's lives.

To Sam Pope with KGB Productions: I am proud to be considered one of your clients and friends. You have an amazing eye for the camera and excellent video production skills. I'm excited to watch your business explode.

To the University of Utah Hospital, specifically Dr. Meic Schmidt: Your medical expertise, dedication, and personal sacrifice for your profession make you the top neurosurgeon in the business. Thank you for being the best at what you do.

To Tyler, "Trent Jensen," and the Jackson Hole EMS: Thank you for your dedication and commitment to your jobs. You save lives. I am honored to be among the people you have saved.

Most importantly, I want to thank God. The credit is truly all Yours. I do not know all of the reasons why this has happened, and I may never know, but there is no doubt in my mind that You have been actively involved. I *know* that You have worked a miracle. I do not know why You saved me, but it is very clear to me that You acted in grace, love, and mercy on my behalf. *I'm all in.*

red arrow

Red Arrow Media is a company of media professionals with diverse, cosmopolitan backgrounds and a wealth of experience, all united by our desire to create, produce, and distribute excellent literary texts and other media worldwide. We offer a comprehensive menu of publishing services and specialize in helping both budding and seasoned authors find their literary voice, write and edit their texts, and create powerful and pleasing interior and exterior designs. We also connect our authors with a plethora of other media services, from printing and distribution to bookselling, website development, publicity campaigns, photography, and video production.